I FORGIVE

I Forgive

by Philip Schmucker

Copyright © 1994 by Philip Schmucker
All Rights Reserved
Printed in the United States of America
First Edition
Published by Express Motivations
Fraser, MI 48026

Design By: Diane Harper
Edited by: Edward Penét

INTRODUCTION BY MARK VICTOR HANSEN

BREAKING THROUGH

The commercial says: "...that with a name like Schmucker, it's got to be good."

With a name like Phil Schmucker this book on a miracle transformation has got to be good.

Phil is an amazing man. He has a captivating, heartwarming story of overcoming obstacles, pain and the frailty of a body that is a continuous learning experience.

I have known, admired and appreciated Phil for many years. He is a super student, thinker and forever smiling friend.

Phil frequently attends my lectures in Metro-Detroit. He has a brilliant, absorbent mind. He is always present-time available and drinks in all the love, light and laughter that exists in my seminars and the ones he attends of my colleagues. My colleague speakers have come to recognize, remember and respect Phil. This admiration comes because Phil is incarcerated in a physical body that is slightly controlled, yet he has obviously mastered his spirit, mind and body and prevails with joy and bliss. He is always friendly, sincere, helpful and 100% the active, dynamic cheerleader-cum-student. I am proud to call him my friend.

Enjoy reading his book *I Forgive...Miracle of Transformation* and get your own miracle.

Mark Victor Hansen
Co-Author: *Chicken Soup for the Soul*
Author: *Dare To Win*

ACKNOWLEDGMENTS

Over the three years it has taken to write this book, there are many people I want to acknowledge for their support. There are so many! Beginning at the moment of inspiration, Dr. Raymond Genick gave me my start as a public speaker. It wasn't two weeks after I told him my about crazy idea to be a motivational speaker that I spoke before one of his business entrepreneurship classes at Wayne State University. The motivational speaking goal was expanded to include writing, when my friend, Jerry Stanecki, recognized the writer in me. The decision to abandon my typewriter and to buy a computer was a challenge in itself. Alex LaVole and the staff at InaComp Computer had the patience to walk me through the selection as well as the learning process. With word processing help again through Ray Genick, I remember everyone's amazement at how fast I learned to use this machine. I also cannot forget Gary Lalonde who has become my dearest friend and support over the last three years. He taught me almost everything I know about Neuro-linguistic Programming. During the times when my computer was in danger of being cast into oblivion, Gary's supportive telephone voice rescued it.

A very special thanks is owed to my many friends at the Church Of Today, some of whom played a direct role in my transformation. Guy Lynch, the current Senior Minister, is always there to help when I encounter my Black Knight of the Soul. In the beginning, it was the late Jack Boland, founder of the Church Of Today, who saw my creative spirit, drew it out of me and nurtured it. Following Jack's death, Michael Murphy continued seeing for me what I couldn't see for myself. In addition to, these are other church staff and a long list of invaluable friends who I cannot completely list here. Other Church Of Today members to whom I owe a debt of gratitude are Ralph Grzecki and Greg M. Ralph, who was a part of my life for a brief time only and gave me a phone number that started this book process rolling. Greg M., my A.A. sponsor, spent many long hours with me as I faced my Black Knight.

The next three people to be acknowledged remain the most important people in my life. There were times during my writing when I saw no way that this dream could ever come true, and times when I didn't know who I was or what I really wanted. As the story unfolded, everything to make this book a reality came to be. After one phone call to David Lindsey, Diane Harper came into my life. She read the manuscript and was excited to see the book become a reality. Diane asked her writer and producer friend, Edward Penét, to read it. He became my editor. When the need came for money to launch the editing and production process, God drew Emmett Webb back into my life. As I re-read the account of how this book came into being, I cannot ignore how the processes of visualization and self-acceptance brought all of the necessary people and other elements together to help make this book a reality.

Two other important people in my life are my former wife, Joyce Schmucker, and my friend, Sally Charles. When it came time to write the story of our relationship, I first asked Joyce to write her version of what happened. I used her recollections as the basis for my telling our story. Writing about our relationship helped heal many old wounds. For the first time in my life, I understood her feelings concerning family, marriage, sex, alcohol and more. What Joyce could not get me to see when we were married was that I needed to love myself. At that time, I not only felt unworthy, but any positive direction I may have exhibited in my life was a show — an act. Actually, I felt deeply wounded by life and was very angry. My anger destroyed my marriage and very nearly cost me my life.

To teach me self-love so I could begin to become the person God created me to be, God brought Sally Charles into my life. As the book closes, I am deep in my transformation. It was heightened in every aspect as I attempted to build a relationship with Sally. Her greatest lesson for me was to look beyond my physical body and the limitations I created for myself. She demonstrated to me that the "Handicapped" label wasn't noticeable until I focused upon it. It is me, myself, who confines me within my assumed limits and so-called "dis-abilities." Through my struggles to build a relationship with Sally, I also learned the difference between unconditional love and co-dependence. For these lessons, I am very grateful to her. She will always have a special place in my heart.

During my time as a member of the Church Of Today, I have learned how important it is to tell someone what your are going to do. Vocalizing aloud and publishing your dreams is a powerful motivator — as well as an absolute necessity for making thoughts come alive. As I learned to visualize my dreams, I took walks through model homes. One dream home in particular was in my neighborhood. Within minutes after I walked, in I was telling the realtor I was visualizing my dreams while I was writing a book that would launch my writing and speaking career. For a time, I made these trips to this model three times a week. The realtor, Frank Valenti, and I soon became friends. He began to cut out newspaper articles about me, displaying them on the walls of the model. He would tell the customers who I was and that I was writing a great book. His daughter, Josie, wrote about me and my short stories at school. It is through visualization that I build my dreams, accomplish my goals, and build a network of valuable friends. Frank is only one example. This book cites many more.

Lastly, I would be remiss if I didn't thank the following friends. First, the office staff members of Hanover Grove Apartments, where I live; including Cathy Raymond, Michelle Valent, and Veronica Kitrys, who allowed me to use their copier many times during the writing of this manuscript. Thank you, as well, to the staff of Ken's Printing, including Sharon Massie, Jason Hill and Tari Martin, who drilled and collated countless manuscript pages. Lastly, my friend and master mechanic, Michael Siedlak. Michael had absolutely nothing to do with writing this book; however, he has gone to the limits innumerable times to keep my Volkswagen running for many years. For a person like myself, who can so easily trap himself within his limitations, my car is my freedom. If not for Michael, I could have never kept myself on my road to success.

Thank you — all.

EXCELSIOR!

DEDICATION

TO MY SOULMATE

In the process of putting this book together, I have wrestled with the dedication. Now that the book is complete and I can see how my story unfolds to this point in my life, I accept that I am still searching for the spirit with whom I began this journey some time ago.

To you, I dedicate this book.

There were many moments in my life when I thought I had found you, but I was mistaken. I truly believe you are in my life as I write this paragraph. I am learning to create my own reality. Only you, working within God's plan, can create a reality for yourself.

With God as my strength, whoever and wherever you are, my heart and soul will always be open to your communication and love.

Phil

CONTENTS

PROLOGUE	xiii
DAD WAS A DREAMER	1
PHILIP'S ORDEAL	17
YOU? A WRITER?	33
DADDY IS DYING	51
DREADING THE FUTURE	69
NEW OPPORTUNITIES	87
ONLY TWO CLIENTS	109
YOU'RE NEVER SATISFIED	125
THIS IS MARRIAGE?	141
THE TOY TRAIN BUSINESS CHANGES	159
FANTASTIC IDEA	175
THE PARTY	191
LOOSE ENDS AND A NEW BEGINNING	207

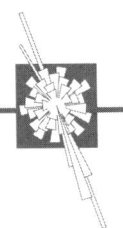

PROLOGUE

HEAVEN OR HELL

Physicists theorize there are precise moments in our universe where the question "What time is it?" answers itself: "Now!" Such a precise moment occurs where time, space, mass and energy all intersect in what physicists term a singularity. It's also known as a "black hole." The concept of the "Eternal Now" is an ancient idea conceived by mystics and spiritual cultures to express God. The idea of the past and future swallowed by the present is a fantastic concept, impossible to imagine. For those of us born with physical or learning disabilities, each moment of life is an ever-present "Now." An eternal hell. A bliss unending. Fire. Ice. Grief. Joy.

A child in me imagines Heaven "up there" in that eternal "Now," where God guides creation from a spacious Command Center, panelled in oak and trimmed in gold. Enormous in stature with a full white beard, like Santa Claus in a white tuxedo, working at a computer only God could have imagined, God designs unique challenges and opportunities for everything in creation to love and be loved. Planet Earth and its creatures are no exception.

James, the butler, approaches God's workstation with a carafe of fresh coffee. The computer whirs at full tilt. Files, disks, flash memory chips and printouts clutter His console.

"Fresh coffee, Sir?" James inquires.

"Yes, thank you, James. Arabica. How appropriate."

"One of your very favorite blends, as I recall, Sir."

"And quite apropos, since I've been working with Earth files all morning."

"Yes, Sir."

"I am committed to find the right pair ..."

"You always do that, Sir," James quietly interrupts.

God's computer slips into idle mode. Angel fish swim across the screen. James pours a fresh mug for God, Who closes a file, takes the mug with a silent nod, then walks to a huge bay window, which overlooks His universe.

"Of all of the galaxies, James ..."

"Sir?"

"... that one planet ..."

"Earth, Sir?" half-listening as he shines a drop of coffee from the toe of his right shoe on the back of his left trouser leg. In God's own silence, James looks up in full attention.

"... understanding, compassion, love, James. They simply don't get it.

"No, Sir."

"Ask Patricia to step in, please."

"Right, Sir."

Patricia bounds into the Control Center before James can pivot to exit. Patricia confidently sweeps past James with two file folders, which she briskly hands to God.

"Took a little imagination, but here you are, Sir. In my opinion, the files of the two best qualified souls for the Earth assignment." She smiles, quietly proud of her results.

God accepts the files from Patricia. "Hopefully, they will choose to accept."

"Only you know that, Sir," she smiles.

"Yes. Send for him, please. I'd like to personally ..."

"Sir, I've already taken the liberty. He's outside in the lobby waiting. Peter is presently in session with the other."

"Very good. Then, ask him to come in, please, Patricia."

Both James and Patricia exit.

The Mission

God turns toward the door as it re-opens. "Hello, my friend."

As this soul reaches out to shake God's hand, God opens His arms to embrace him. While they embrace warmly, God whispers, "I have a great favor to ask of you. It is a challenge few in heaven would ever consider, even as a supreme favor."

"If You ask, it must be possible, so how could I refuse?"

"My dear soul, what I am offering you is a challenge that must be chosen of your own free will. It is not a commandment. Please ..." God motions for the soul to be seated in a white velvet overstuffed chair. "Do you know the term suffering?".

"I understand suffering to be the ignorance of incarnate beings," the soul responds. "To know Good and Evil is considered both a blessing and a curse by the Enlightened Ones. For most of us, it is a deep mystery that cannot be truly known, only experienced within the thankfully forgiving limits of space and time."

"You remember being such an incarnate?" God asks.

"Yes. Many times. How horrible and at the same time, how wonderful each lifetime was. Each unique. Yet, each the same. And after each, an even more wonderful reunion with You. I learned much. And in the most recent lifetime, I was joined by my soulmate," the soul beams. In fact, the very thought of his soulmate breaks his focus on the conversation.

"Well!" God muses loudly to bring the conversation back on track. As He gestures out through the bay window, suddenly, the panorama of the universe shimmers into an electric rainbow of dancing colors, then shatters into dozens of moving picture images of a passing lifetime somewhere in the universe, or at least, in God's plan. The imagery is so compelling, it draws the visiting soul from his chair toward the window.

God continues, "My dear soul, this is an outline for a life to be lived on the planet Earth. With your help it will complete itself."

Almost immediately the soul recoils in horror. "This is not a well child. His family, teachers, even his doctors, all abuse him! They shame him! How can they blame him for his tragedy?"

"That is yet to be understood," God proposes aloud.

"Of course he is blameless!" the soul complains. He almost runs from one image to the others in the panorama, motioning and pointing with great excitement as he speaks. "In fact, aside from his tortured appearance, I see he can be a man of great accomplishments, overcoming many obstacles to be an inspiration to others."

"And what of his capacity for love?" God asks deliberately.

"Like all of Your creation, he is capable of giving and receiving love. But the poor devil won't have an easy time of it. And this is?" The soul pauses at the image of a smiling young woman.

"You may remember her. She may break this soul's heart," God muses, looking for a response out of the corner of His eye.

"Yes. He's certainly the type who takes everything to heart."

"I could make him less vulnerable," God considers.

"He'll need all the help he can get to survive childhood, much less young adulthood, and then to marry her!"

"Well, can I count on you, then?" God asks outright.

"Him? Me?" The soul backpedals from the images, which continue to change as quickly as thoughts and fears race through his mind.

God's arm around him calms him, instantly. God guides him to sit in the chair, then turns it slowly to face the images once again.

"A few more details, perhaps. But just a few."

The soul is quickly attentive. "He speaks to multitudes and he inspires many with his books and tapes!"

"He should, in fact, become widely read, which would bring him and his love material comfort later in life," God adds.

"Wow! A cashier's check for ... Oh, I missed it! For how much?"

God continues, "And speaking of his love ..."

"That's her! That's my soulmate! He knows my soulmate in his life?"

"With a stroke of the pen," God smiles. "It can all be arranged."

The soul looks at God, then to the screen, which is awash again with stars, then back to God. "But, what happens with her in her life? Her eyes expressed so much shame and suffering!"

God steps forward and speaks gently. "My dear soul, in this probable scenario, each of you will be challenged with different forms of physical and emotional terror, but to similar degrees. Each of you will individually struggle through a recovery from blame and shame, as you put it, again, in unique ways and under very different circumstances. "The answer to the question you are thinking is, yes. The potential exists, as never before, to love one another."

The soul sighs with gratitude.

"But only when you are both ready to receive will you be reunited. Before that time, a reunion would be too painful."

Without hesitation, the soul speaks matter-of-factly. "I see two entire human lifetimes of pain. More than half of both lives spent in solitary mental and physical terror, with no real possibility of love, given or received. Then…perhaps…there may occur a double transformation, two miraculous recoveries. And only then, the potential reunion of soulmates."

Nodding in agreement, God responds, "Remember, potential has the same root as potency. It is an extraordinary pair of lives I propose for the two of you. It's a one in a ... no, actually, a two in two million opportunity!"

"Isn't there another pair ... or some other possibilities? Besides, how can I decide for the two of us?"

"I'm not asking that of you. In fact, your soulmate was briefed at the same time as you and is ready to help you make a joint decision." God turns to the intercom, "Patricia ..."

"Send her in now, Sir?" Patricia intuits.

"Yes, Patricia."

Immediately, the Command Center door opens, and the soulmate enters. The powerful energy between the two spirits is magnified in God's presence. In their deep union, which mirrors all that is God, they review the life imagery outlined for them.

In peace, they speak to God: "Let it be."

God blesses them with His embrace: "I am with you."

In the "Now" of their love, the two spirits separate in a cloud of knowing. All thought compresses and hollows in a tunnel of light. Then, darkness. And the rhythmic washing of waves.

dad was a dreamer

It was one of those early April-in-Michigan days, when the southwest breeze is warm, like a lover's caress. A man in his early twenties paced across the plot of land, where he was about to construct his dream castle for his bride. Six feet tall, 220 pounds of self-made individual; he took pride in his native genius that he could build or fix anything. It was on this land, this little piece of heaven, he planned to raise his family and live happily ever after.

Long before Clarence Schmucker had ever met Lorraine Zehnder, he spent many long nights dreaming his dream, drawing the plans for his castle into the wee hours of the morning on his mother's dining room table. It never occurred to him that he had no training as an architect or a draftsman, or that he used only a pencil and a ruler. Clarence Schmucker could never allow anything or anyone to keep him from accomplishing his dream. He'd been walking his land near Mound Road and Eleven Mile for several hours, but it was mid-morning before he heard the growing sound of the lumber truck slowly make its way up Mound.

Michigan was still soft with the spring thaw. Small puddles stood along the road. The driver had taken the time to steer his rig carefully along these country roads to keep his heavy load from sinking into the soft spots that crept out now and again from either side of the greening fields.

As the truck neared the property, Clarence ran out to the driver, gesturing and yelling, "Pull 'er back in there!"

The driver squinted out over the open field, then shouted back. "Can't put this load in there today, Mister. It's a better 'an even chance she'll get stuck. I'll drop it all right here by the shoulder, where the ground's harder and drier."

"If you know how to drive this damn thing, you won't get stuck!" Clarence shouted back. "Besides, I don't want my lumber on the road, where some bastards can come along and help themselves to a five finger discount!"

As the driver assessed the situation, Clarence impatiently moverd closer to the truck. "Look. I want this entire load back *there* where your dispatcher *agreed* I could have it." Then, softening his tone, "If you *do* get stuck, I'll pull you out."

The driver peered toward a row of pines and noticed a little '37 Ford pickup truck nearly hidden in the tall scrub. He shook his head.

Clarence didn't lose a beat. "Look, you've got my paid-for lumber, and you'll drop it where I want it, or I'll call the yard and tell your bosses where *they* can stick it."

The driver imagined the nightmare he might be getting into, but he grit his teeth, slammed the truck into reverse, and backed the load across the soft earth, stopping exactly where Clarence directed. The sound and feel of the soft earth under his feet didn't at all reassure the driver he'd done the right thing, but he pulled on his heavy gloves and reached to pull himself up onto the flatbed. He wasn't thinking about where Clarence was at the moment, so it surprised him to see Clarence's outstretched hand reaching down to hoist him up. The driver was now shaking hands with a one-of-a-kind man. A man who'd work next to any other honest working man. A man who, though he was the customer, was not ashamed to pitch in, stride for stride, pound for pound, hour for hour.

The two men finished the job without exchanging a word. Or, if a word was spoken, it didn't come from Clarence Schmucker. With a simple nod of thanks, the driver handed over the shipping bill, climbed into his rig, and started it up. By this time, all thoughts of the soft spring earth had been forgotten. But when he began to let out the clutch, he could feel that every tire had been drawn into the soft soil under the weight of the load. He carefully eased out the clutch and the truck inched forward. Inches became feet, which became yards. The driver never paused, even as the truck hit the hard-packed road.

As the rig made the turn onto the road, Clarence broke his self-imposed silence and shouted after the driver with typical sarcasm, "Thought you'd *never* get that damn truck outta here! I gotta house to build, you know!" The driver didn't hear him, though he waved.

In the late afternoon air, the sound of the empty rumbling rig carried over the fallow fields long after the outline of the flatbed lost itself in the tree line.

Honey, I'm pregnant

Working across town and living at his folks with his young wife were motives, over the following months, to bring his castle to the point where it was weather-tight and livable. The move came during the unforgiving muggy heat of early August. Without much to furnish it completely, the interior appeared even more mammoth than its generous design actually was. Clarence called it "growing room."

From the road, you saw the wide front porch, which one day would have a swing for summer evenings. Passing by, going north, you couldn't help but notice the large bay window, which was off the dining room. Inside, the spacious living room had a large fireplace and stone hearth. And of course, it boasted a large kitchen with wide counters and plenty of cupboard space.

Lorraine was prepared to make up for the lost time, having lived their first three years at his mother's. As she unpacked in the kitchen, her own thoughts and dreams were always interrupted by Clarence's dreams about building a family, starting with a first-born son. If a son would make her man happy, a *son* is what Lorraine was committed to provide

Late one September Saturday morning, after Clarence had been out framing his new garage since dawn, Lorraine brought out a steaming cup of black coffee and a thick slice of buttered, fresh-baked bread. He noticed her smile the moment she left the porch, but he kept on working, following her out of the corner of his eye. She had both eyes on him, however, across the entire side yard, until she reached the foot of his ladder.

Lorraine set the coffee and plate of bread on his weathered work table, then looked back up at him, shielding her eyes from the bright sun. Clarence kept banging away without pause. He never did turn to her, look down, or say thanks for the coffee and bread. She continued to stare up at him for a minute or so, then called up to him, "Clarence! I'm pregnant! I'm going to give you that son of yours!" Without waiting for a reply, she turned toward the house and disappeared through the back porch screen door.

Moments later, Lorraine's brother Leo, a master butcher, pulled up the driveway. "Hey, Smuck!" he shouted up to Clarence. "Ma told me the good news! Congratulations!"

"Come here to help or just visit your sister?" Clarence droned in counterpoint to the steady rhythm of his hammer.

"Little of both, maybe. Say, you two found a doctor out here yet? Ma's first grandson's gotta have the best!"

Clarence came down the ladder, but only to fill his pouch with fresh spikes out of an open keg. "Women been having babies for ten thousand years, Leo, without running to a doctor. Why should Lorraine be any different? Besides, who the hell's gonna pay our doctor bills? You?"

Leo's eyes followed Clarence's boots up the ladder. "Aw, Smuck, I just thought, with something like this you would want Lorraine and the baby to have the best care is all. I'm gonna go in and say hi." As he turned, like many times before, Leo felt he just didn't ever seem to know what to say to Clarence. That side of the family never did understand Clarence. Or maybe it was the other way around.

Leo snuck into the house and tiptoed up behind Lorraine, who was busy stocking her new cupboards. "Boo!"

"Oh ma' God! Leo! You can't sneak up behind a pregnant woman like that!" When his face fell with worry, she laughed. Then, they spun in an embrace like two giddy children. "You been drinking this early in the day?" she chided.

"Nah! Sure is a nice house Smuck built for you – both." Leo took a cup from the new cupboard. "See?" he made a point about drinking coffee. He walked to the stove where Lorraine was keeping a coffee pot warm. "Why a man who can give you all this won't bother to find you a good doctor is…"

Lorraine cut him off. "You know how he is. You know he's going to do this thing *his* way. In *his* time. We've got time," she said, patting her flat stomach.

"Maybe, you shouldn't have married the man," Leo mumbled.

"I love him, Leo. And I always will!"

"Sorry, Sis, I don't want to meddle. I just want what's best for you and my new nephew."

Lorraine kissed him lightly on the cheek. "You know, I watched Ma have you and Carl without problems. She went on to have seven of us at home. *without* a doctor."

Leo smiled and headed toward the back porch door. "Thanks for the coffee. I'll go see what O' Smuck is up to. That man of yours never wants to relax. Work, work, work."

Straightening a dish cloth, Lorraine replied, "He wouldn't know what to do with himself if he wasn't building or fixing something."

That night, after Lorraine finished the dishes, she went into the living room to relax with her crocheting. Clarence, who never would be one to do "woman's work" had left the table for his favorite chair, the evening paper and a beer. As Lorraine got herself organized, Clarence folded his paper, finished his beer, then walked to the couch and sat beside her.

He put his arm around her shoulder and said, "I've though about it. And I've decided to take you to see Ma's doctor, Doctor Woods." Without looking up, Lorraine stopped what she was doing.

"I'm thinking, Ma trusts the old guy, so he'll probably do fine. I'll call tomorrow from Ma's and make an appointment." Satisfied he had done the right thing, Clarence returned to his chair and his paper. Lorraine felt safe in that moment. She quietly took a deep breath and went on with her needlework.

Dinner At Ma's

During the next seven months, the whole world changed. America became involved in World War II. Home building and, as a result, Clarence's wet plastering trade came to a grinding stop. But an even greater disappointment was the Army's discovery of Clarence's heart murmur, likely caused by the Scarlet Fever he suffered as a child. Though he wouldn't be able to serve his country on active duty, he soon came to see this as a blessing in disguise that allowed him to remain at home, keep working on his house, and see his son born. In no time, everything had settled itself into a routine. A civilian job as a security guard at a Navy Ordinance Plant brought in a paycheck. In addition, visits with Dr. Woods were followed by a quiet dinner at Clarence's mother's.

The last visit before the baby was due proved to be anything but routine, however. As Clarence sat restless in the waiting room, thinking of all of the things that needed doing, Dr. Woods discovered Lorraine not only had elevated blood pressure, but also albumin in her blood.

"What does this mean?" she asked, concerned only for her baby.

"No real need to worry. Just take care of yourself. You and the baby should be fine. Plan to see me on the due date, if the baby hasn't come by then. Don't you worry," Dr. Woods advised.

Almost at the same time, Clarence's mother felt something, perhaps a premonition similar to the one Clarence's step-father had sensed months earlier, the day Lorraine announced the news. When Clarence and Lorraine arrived at his mother's, she was waiting for them at the front door. But before she could say a word, Clarence's eleven-year-old sister, Dorothy, slipped past to greet them.

"Can I hold the baby, Lorraine? Can I, Clarence? Please?"

In an obviously worried state, Clarence snapped, "Can't you even wait till the kid gets here first!" With that he rushed past Dorothy and his mother with a cold, "When do we eat, Ma?"

His mother felt his concern and saw it quite clearly in Lorraine's eyes.

"Come in, Lorraine," she smiled. "And you!" she said after Clarence, "You watch how you talk to your sister!"

His step-father's entrance through the back door minutes later was the usual signal for the family to eat. No one spoke as the food was passed. Everyone always waited for Daddy Hennicken to start the table conversation.

At long last, Daddy asked Clarence, "How be it go at Doctor Woods, today?"

Everyone stopped eating, waiting for Clarence to respond.

"Fine!" Clarence answered with too much emotion.

Daddy now knew he had been right all along. "You be take good care my grandson and his mother," Daddy said not challenging Clarence's words.

"Sure, Daddy. I'll take good care of them both."

After dinner, while the women tended to the dishes, Clarence and his father sat on the front porch in one of the first warm evenings of the spring season. Nothing more was said between them about doctors or babies. Later on the porch, as Lorraine and Clarence pulled away from the house, Daddy turned to Ma. "Mama, something not feel right."

Mama said, "I saw a look in Lorraines eyes when they came in. Something is not what it should be. She said Doctor Woods said she had high blood pressure and albumin in her blood." Mama shrugged and sighed.

Daddy continued to stare down the street, as if he could still follow his son's car through the night.

Mama began again, "She said Doctor Woods said not to worry. 'Take it easy' Doctor Woods told her. Come in to see him if the baby is not on time, doctor say. That is all she said to me."

"So," Daddy sighed, "we go to bed."

Something Goes Wrong

After four weeks, on the day the baby was due, Clarence and Lorraine dutifully returned to Dr. Woods, who expressed more serious concern. "I certainly don't like the looks of things. The sooner this baby is born,

Lorraine, the better for the both of you. If the baby isn't born in four days, we'll induce labor. Do you understand, Lorraine?"

Lorraine nodded, but she didn't understand the implications.

Reacting worse, Clarence didn't know what to do to make things all right. Nothing but questions kept going through his mind. "Wasn't there something to fix Lorraine's blood pressure? And her albumin, couldn't something be done about that? What did this mean for Lorraine? Would she have more children. And what about this baby? Doctor Woods must know what he's doing. We've got to trust Doctor Woods to do what's right. After all, me, my brother, and my three sisters were brought into the world by Doctor Woods. Hey, just four more days, and then I'll have a son!"

Four days later, they returned to Dr. Woods at 6 p.m. Injections were given every half hour, until Lorraine's water broke at 10 p.m. Dr. Woods sent them on to the hospital. After 14 hours of labor, Lorraine was still not fully dilated. With Caesarean delivery ruled out due to Lorraine's high blood pressure, Dr. Woods began the attempt to pull the baby out with forceps. The more pressure he applied, however, the worse it became for Lorraine.

"Time is against this baby," he thought, as he considered tucking the baby back into the womb and turning it to deliver it feet first.

Again he tried forceps, but they cut into the baby's forehead and temple. With nearly all hope lost for a live birth, and only in consideration for Lorraine, Dr. Woods pushed the baby back into her womb, turned it, and took it feet first. The tiny body was limp, its head indented and lacerated.

"My God, it's alive!" the doctor marvelled, handing the baby to a nurse, immediately shifting his focus to Lorraine.

The nurse rushed the infant to the nursery, where it was placed under intensive care. Live birth. Philip…John…Schmucker. Male. Caucasian. 6 pounds. 15 ounces. 21 inches.

Clarence was pacing in the waiting room with the other expectant fathers when Dr. Woods rushed in and physically yanked Clarence into the hall.

"Clarence! You must go upstairs immediately and give us blood for your wife and child."

Clarence blew his stack before Dr. Woods could point him to the elevator. "What's going on? What the hell have you done with my wife and baby, you incompetent son-of-a-bitch!"

"Clarence! No time! You must do as I say! Get hold of yourself, man!" Dr. Woods held his ground, and Clarence took off in a panic. As he ran, he thought that whatever was happening now was neither the "snap" he thought it would be for Lorraine, nor was it the great and glorious moment he'd always dreamed for himself. "Child!? Boy or girl? Woods didn't say! Lorraine! This isn't a dream. It's a nightmare!"

Late that night, exhausted, afraid, and weakened after donating blood, Clarence returned as arranged to his parents' house. He knew none of the details, not even the sex of his child. Worse for his parents, who tried their best to comfort him, he expressed only frustration and fear. The family could only wait.

Homecoming

Nine days later, Lorraine gently and curiously unwrapped Philip's blankets on Clarence's mother's couch. All the time she was in the hospital, she had never been allowed to hold Philip. She hadn't nursed him, because she was too weak, and so no one had instructed her how to nurse. Today was the first time she had picked Philip up by herself for all to see. Philip's eyes were open, though he laid totally still. His head was obviously misshapen and still badly bruised from the forceps.

Gathered around the mother and child, family members were dazed. No one spoke. The new Grandpa, his hands clasped behind his back, looked in. "Iey-yei!" he said, sadly turned away, and left the room. Clarence had already grabbed two beers from the fridge and was headed out to the front porch. Grandma sent Dorothy to her room, then took Lorraine and her baby to the kitchen to show her how to nurse.

Clarence looked at the empty beer bottle in his hand. He didn't remember drinking it. He opened the second bottle on a gap between the porch bricks. He remembered a time when some big boys down the block came by and broke his new toy.

His step-father reappeared through the front door with two beers. "What you do, Clarence?" he asked, taking a puff on a cigarette.

"Hell, Daddy, I don't know." Clarence said, his attention drawn to the drone of the yellow street light and the growing cloud of insects attracted to its eerie glow.

His step-father opened one of the beers in the same gap in the bricks. "For these many months, I know it not right. But I can do nothing. So, I wait."

Clarence knew his step-father was urging patience. "I don't want to wait, Daddy. I wanted a *son*. Now, I *have* a son." Tears filled his eyes. "But, he doesn't *move*, Daddy. He doesn't even *cry!*"

"So, we wait. We see what comes."

HE'S OUR KID

Two weeks after bringing their new baby home, Philip cried for the first time. Not long after, Lorraine's father died, leaving Lorraine's mother alone in a summer cabin on Bass Lake, near Walled Lake, Michigan. Originally from Millington, a little town East of Frankenmuth, Michigan, the family moved from their cottage into a rental house in town each winter. Clarence offered to build an attic apartment in their house for Lorraine's mother so she could be with family while Leo was off to war. It was also another major project in which Clarence could lose himself.

Lorraine's mother moved in to the roughed-in attic apartment just before Christmas of that year, and she stayed for several years, later joined by Leo after the war. However, friction between Clarence and his in-laws eventually led him to offer to winterize their lake cottage, a project he eagerly launched the following spring.

It was no secret. Everyone knew there was something wrong with Philip. But this was the early 1940s, and there seemed to be no place or no one to turn to for help. Making matters worse were Clarence's nightly battles with Lorraine's mother. While she watched Lorraine play with Philip, her mother couldn't help herself. She'd speak so her voice would carry no matter where

Clarence was in the house.

"Lorraine, Philip is almost eight months old now. By now he should be able to hold his head up alone."

"I know, Mother."

"Well, I think it's about time you and Clarence find a doctor to tell you two what is wrong. You can't spend the rest of your lives living with this ... uncertainty," she'd go on.

"Yes, Mother."

This would continue until Clarence would decide he'd had enough. He would come into the room, glare at his mother-in-law, but speak only to Lorraine.

"Lorraine, will you tell your mother to stop nagging us! He's our kid, and if anything is going to be done with him, we will be the ones to decide what to do and when to do it! Not her! Not anyone else!"

Grandma would be quiet for a moment, then come right back with, "Clarence, if you love your son the way you profess, you wouldn't just let him lay there the way he is. Look at him! The poor little dear."

As time passed, Lorraine's mother continued to work as a sales clerk at a local department store. And when Leo returned from the war, he picked up the family's butchering trade at a local A&P. The end of the war also brought Clarence back into the building trade, as the pre-fabricated housing industry boomed in Michigan.

THE SEARCH BEGINS

Whatever may have motivated Clarence to finally take action regarding Philip's condition, he did so at long last, when Philip was nearing three. Because he still had not spent the money to have a telephone installed in their home, he stopped at his mother's one morning on his way in to work and placed a call to Dr. Woods for the name of a doctor who would examine Philip. Dr. Woods referred him to Dr. Golden, a pediatrician.

Following a 20-minute preliminary examination of Philip, the doctor said he would like to see them in his office.

"Mr. and Mrs. Schmucker, I have given your son a thorough examination. There isn't much I can tell you that you probably don't already surmise. Your son will never walk or talk. My best advice to you is to place Philip in an institution where he will be cared for. Live your lives. In time you'll forget about all of this. You might even get on with a family. I'm sorry, but there's nothing more I can do."

After an awkward silence, Clarence exploded. "What in the name of ... what the hell are you telling us? He's my only son! Damned if I'll put my only son in an institution! You lousy son-of-a-bitch, saying that in front of my wife."

Lorraine broke into heavy sobs the moment Clarence opened fire. On the way home, he was quiet. And for the moment, her sadness, more dark and deeply felt than ever before, ceased its overflow.

As occasional doctor visits occurred over the next year, Philip became aware that there were things about him that made his mother sad and made his father angry, things that he didn't understand, but things that he somehow knew couldn't be fixed.

An idea Lorraine's mother had was to take Philip to a chiropractor. It was several months before the subject came up again, brought up by their neighbor, Floyd, who liked to visit Philip and play with him.

"Careful how you mention that to Clarence, Floyd," Lorraine cautioned. "You know how hot he can get about that."

"You want Philip to spend the rest of his life like this? You want to spend the rest of your life taking care of him, when he's a grown man, and he can't walk, talk, or hardly swallow?"

Floyd grabbed a couple of beers and went over to where Clarence was busy working on the house. "Hey, Smuck, take a beer break?"

"Yah! Sounds good. Thanks, Floyd."

"You know how much I like that boy of yours?" Floyd eyed Clarence carefully. "Well, I was just over by Philip, when the thought came to me. Chiropractors do great things for adults. Maybe there's one who could do something for a little boy like Philip? Ever think of taking Philip to a chiropractor, Smuck?"

Clarence looked Floyd in the eye, then took long drink of his beer. "All the dead ends," he said shaking his head. "I'm not saying I've given up, Floyd. Just, there's been a lot of dead ends."

Clarence stared up at the clouds, as he finished off the bottle. The sound of a hand mower chattered somewhere. From across the yard, Lorraine could see Floyd had made an impression. Floyd waited until Clarence looked at him before he continued.

"You think about it, Clarence. But I got the name and number of a real good chiropractor. You let me know when you're ready, Clarence."

Clarence was no fool. He wouldn't refuse an honest chance to help his son. And he was willing to risk the further disappointment that might come.

Sadly, it was another disappointment. All the chiropractor did was diagnose Philip's apparent curvature of the spine. After six months of painful adjustments, Clarence could see no change and decided to stop pouring his money into another bottomless pit.

The Search Ends

By the spring of 1945, Clarence had finally converted his mother-in-law's cottage into a year-round home. Lorraine's mother and Leo moved, allowing Clarence to reclaim his castle for himself and his family. Later that summer, Clarence and Lorraine enjoyed a weekend driving vacation, one of several he and Lorraine took each year. They drove up north to visit his cousin, Judy, a nurse, and her family. He hadn't seen them since before Philip was born.

As the two families shared stories, Clarence naturally told his story about Philip's birth. Judy carefully watched Philip while she listened. Stopping Clarence in mid-sentence, Judy matter-of-factly said, "Clarence, I think I know exactly what's wrong with Philip."

Lorraine handed Philip to Judy, who held him on her lap and carefully observed his movements. "I think Philip has what's called Cerebral Palsy."

"What the hell is that?" Clarence asked.

"They say it's often caused by one or a combination of injuries to the brain during birth. I'm no expert, but there's a doctor in Detroit who specializes in this."

A long and frustrating search was about to pay off. As he drove home from their trip, Clarence felt like a changed man. He had the name and number in his pocket of a doctor who could fix his son. He called from his mother's right away Monday morning, but the soonest the doctor could see Philip was in two weeks.

A nurse took Philip's history from Clarence and Lorraine, then left them in the examining room to wait for Dr. Joseph Walsh, an orthopedic specialist. Dr. Walsh was in his mid-thirties, stocky, with curly, salt and pepper hair, and wore a suit and vest. Initially, he said nothing, but walked over to where Philip was shivering, lying nude in the cool air on the hard examination table. As the doctor began to gently flex Philip's arms and legs, he spoke.

"My nurse tells me you think your son has Cerebral Palsy."

"Why… er, yes, my cousin up north suggested it might be, whatever it is called and gave me your name." Clarence felt nervous, but sensed that this doctor knew what he was doing.

"Mr. and Mrs, Schmucker, your son definitely has Cerebral Palsy. I'll write it down for you so you can remember it."

Clarence impatiently interrupted, "But will he ever walk or talk?" He and Lorraine were hanging on the doctor's every word.

Dr. Walsh sighed. "I think so … but …"

"Thank God!" Clarence shouted, interrupting again. And he kissed Lorraine. "When? How long? I mean, er, before he walks and talks?" Clarence excitedly asked.

"Mr. Schmucker. Mrs. Schmucker. It won't be that cut and dry. It will be a long time and demand much hard work from the *three* of you, before Philip will walk and talk." Clarence was thinking in terms of weeks, perhaps, a few months. "OK. Well, what do we do first?"

The doctor's prescriptions were clear.

"First, we'll fit Philip with leg braces from his feet up to his knees. He must wear them 24 hours a day. In addition, we'll build a standing table, which will force Philip to stand straight. You see, we have to stretch the tendons, so his legs can straighten as he grows. Let me write a prescription so the hospital supply outlet will build one for you."

"Hell, I can build one better and cheaper," Clarence jumped in.

"Well, if that's what you want to do, I can give you the plans for one."

For Clarence, this was a happy moment. He had answers that filled him with hope he had lost after Philip's birth. Lorraine sat quietly listening, not knowing what to make of it all. She didn't feel hope at all. She heard only something about change and a long-away future. But right now she wanted all of this to be over. She wanted to be home with her baby.

Philip looked at his mother, his father, then at the doctor. Somehow, Philip knew. He could tell his ordeal was about to begin.

philip's ordeal

Philip's ordeal began with metal leg braces and a standing table. His leg braces were pairs of metal rods extending from a collar below each knee to a steel foot plate that held the feet parallel and straight. Philip had these hot and heavy braces strapped to his legs 24 hours a day. The standing table was a 3-foot square wood surface on 18-inch legs. A narrow door in the center of the table opened into an equally narrow boxed-in space.

Philip was lifted with his braces into this box and made to stand several hours each day, while he played supported only by the walls of the box and his braces. Clarence improved the design by adding a wide lip around the perimeter of the table surface to prevent anything from getting away from Philip.

Results, if any, were very slow in coming. Clarence did everything Dr. Walsh prescribed, because he visualized Philip would be cured soon. "Less than two years and he'll be in school! He *has* to walk and talk to go school!" Clarence thought.

As the weeks and months passed, all Clarence noticed were more doctor bills. On each subsequent visit, Dr. Walsh would lend encouragement, but after several months, he said, "You're right, Mr. Schmucker. While, I do see progress, he isn't making the progress he could. But, there *is* something else we can try."

"What's that?" Clarence asked with a mix of interest and wariness.

"There's a hospital out in the country where therapists treat other children just like Philip. They can give Philip the full-time therapy and motivation to walk and communicate that he can't get at home simply playing by himself."

"More damn money," Clarence muttered, thinking about the IRS who had questioned his medical deductions. "It's only money, right?" Clarence said aloud.

"You do want your son to walk?" the doctor put it plainly.

Clarence turned to look out of the window and think.

Lorraine remained silent, keeping her thoughts to herself. She felt Clarence's hope giving way to the fear that Philip might never walk or talk normally. She remembered the time Clarence force-fed Philip a beer. As Philip gagged and coughed, Clarence raged, "He can't even drink beer like a man!" With Philip safely in her arms, she pleaded with Clarence, "You can't expect him to drink beer! He's just a baby! His problems are not his fault!" With that, the balance was restored. Clarence would continue to hope for them both to find a way to fix their son, while Lorraine would carry in her heart their mutual sadness that Philip would never be perfect. Secretly, Lorraine also began to wonder if "drinking beer like a man" would become another issue on top of everything else for Philip, as it was for others in the family.

Clarence turned from the window to look directly at Lorraine. Without taking his eyes from her, he said to Dr. Walsh, "Do it."

THE CHALLENGE

One sunny, cold morning in January, a morning like any other morning for Philip, he was bundled up for a surprise trip in the car. He loved taking trips in the car, because he'd always see a train somewhere along the way. But there was something different about this trip, the quiet way everyone was behaving, and the fact that only one little suitcase was packed. He also sensed a sadness in his mother, that sadness he always felt when he did something to disappoint her.

He saw no trains along the way. After a long time, as the car slowed, then turned, Philip propped himself up to see where they were. He had never seen a place like this. A big brick building with many floors and windows. And inside, the strange faces and the strange odor, like Grandma's laundry soap, only stronger.

Lorraine walked him into a large bedroom that had many beds. She undressed him and, even though it was still day, she put on his pajamas. She said nothing, kissed him, then left the room. Philip lay there shivering on the strange hard bed when, suddenly, a strange older woman dressed all in white with a stiff white pointed hat appeared at his bed, tucked him too snugly under the covers, yanked up the two tall metal sides of this oversized crib, and disappeared into the shadows.

Able only to turn his head from side to side, Philip noticed for the first time that other little people were sleeping in similar beds on either side of him. Elsewhere in the room, a little voice began to cry softly. He had never seen other children before. Awake with fear and loneliness for hours, hoping his Mama and Daddy would come back to take him home, Philip finally succumbed under the weight of his braces and the bed covers and slept. The other little voice stopped crying.

Lorraine came to see him the next morning.

"I _ant go hom_!" he said as Lorraine walked up to his bed.

"Of course, you do, honey." Lorraine lifted him into an old wooden chair with wheels and pushed him out into the hall. Clarence was standing at the far end of the hall near large wooden double doors with windows. "Listen carefully, honey. Daddy says you can come home as soon as you can walk down this hall and meet me and Daddy at those doors when we visit."

The distance appeared impossible to Philip. He wanted to scream out, "Ma! I can't walk! Please don't ask me to do that!" In the swirl of his panic, the train that thundered behind their house early every morning roared into his consciousness. "I _ant _ive tain!" he would shout. And always his mother would say, "Honey, you *can't*." Now, she was saying, "You *must*!" As the memory of one train faded quickly, carrying with it its precious cargo of a child's hopes and desires, a sudden, jarring crash echoed on the siding. Like the coming together of the iron fists that couple two train cars, it was clear for Philip. As who he felt he was *inside* faded with one train, what he was *outside* coupled with reality. Judgment and challenge were one and the same: Walk and we'll all be happy again.

Six months later, on Philip's fourth birthday, two nurses dressed him in his best shorts and polo shirt. All morning he sat at the end of the hall in a little chair with skis his Daddy had made espcially for him and waited for his parents to visit. Just after lunch, as Clarence and Lorraine approached the big wooden and glass double doors at the end of the long hall, he saw them. Twisting carefully off of his chair, he headed out toward them. They stopped at the door and watched. With his hands on the seat of his chair for balance, Philip triumphantly moved down the long corridor. Intense concentration numbed the pain in his little body as he bravely scuffled along on his tiptoes, throwing one braced leg forward at a time.

Although Philip felt he had kept his part of the bargain, his parents did not take him immediately home that day, as they had promised. They had their reasons, but these were dismissed by the mind of a child who had accepted their bargain that this first performance would yield a reality of love and approval.

The Ultimate Price

On the next visit with Dr. Walsh, the doctor expressed amazement. "I must say, Mr. Schmucker, I have never seen a child learn so quickly to walk. Philip's progress is remarkable."

"But he still isn't walking the way he should!" Clarence commented flatly. "I know he can walk better if he wants to."

"Of course he wants to! Give the boy time. Something or someone has really motivated him."

"That was easy," Clarence said. "We just told him he couldn't come home until he walked down the hall."

Immune to the effects of shame-based cruelty, Dr. Walsh went on to note something else in Philip's file. "I just noticed you live outside the Detroit city limits."

"What does that have to do with things?" Clarence asked.

The doctor looked up. "Well, it's high time you and your wife thought about where you're going to send Philip to school."

"OK. But, what does that have to do with where we live?"

"Mr. Schmucker, the only two schools that will take Philip are both in Detroit. To qualify, Philip must live in the city."

The issue caught Clarence completely off-guard. This he had never anticipated. He went ashen. He heard precisely what the Dr. had said, but only Clarence could have instantly felt what supreme cost was being demanded of him. He couldn't speak. In fact, as the examination continued for several more minutes, all further conversation occurred between the doctor and Lorraine.

After they were well on their way home, Clarence unleashed his feelings, directing his rage to the doctor, then to Lorraine, and ultimately to Philip. This was different. Money was not the issue. Now he had been asked to pay the ultimate price.

"It's not good *enough* that I have to work twice as hard as any man to fix this kid! Now I have to abandon the house I built with my own two hands and move into the damn city, just so the little bastard can go to some crippled kids school!"

In sobs, Lorraine begged Clarence to stop yelling. "Oh, honey, don't talk that way in front of Philip! It's not his fault! He didn't do anything!"

Clarence sighed heavily, suppressing his own gut-wrenching feelings. Exhausted by his deeply felt emotions, Clarence drove in silence the rest of the trip home. Lorraine's sobs subsided to quiet tears. All this time, Philip stared out at what he could see over the car door sill. Tops of buildings. Tall, dark wood poles with arms connected by wires. Street lamps. And finally! Open country! The big blue sky, filled with big, white, fleecy clouds! The clouds helped Philip stop wondering why *what* he was had such power to hurt his parents without his wanting to.

A Double Dilemma

Feeling hopeless and helpless, Clarence needed to talk things over with his stepfather. First thing, on his way to his latest job as a wet plasterer with his uncle, Clarence stopped at his parents'. They were at the breakfast table when he entered the back door. His mother saw that he wanted to be alone with his stepfather, so after a "Hello, Ma" and a kiss, she carried her coffee to the front porch.

Clarence took a cup from the cupboard, poured a coffee for himself, then sat at the opposite end of the table from his stepfather.

"What be the matter, Clarence?"

"Yesterday, Philip's doctor told us we'd have to move into Detroit to send Philip to a special school."

"Eie, yie! I tell you to put the boy in a home? Best for the boy. Best for you and Lorraine."

"Daddy! He's my son! My only child! I can't dump him in some place like that. I know he can be *fixed*, so he can live normal. Besides, I don't think Lorraine could live through another childbirth."

"Then, that's it. You must be selling your house."

Clarence felt stiff from his strenuous plastering job. He rolled his left arm, rubbed his left shoulder, took a deep breath, then suddenly couldn't exhale without chest pain. He knew he was feeling tense about a lot of things, but he never had experienced pain like this.

"You OK?" his stepfather asked.

Clarence nodded, and after a few seconds he caught his breath again. "Daddy, I haven't been feeling well these pass few weeks. It's too damn hot and humid to spread plaster, today. I think I'll go back home instead of going to work."

"Maybe you call Doctor Woods. He look at you."

"Oh, I don't know."

His Daddy's sixth sense prompted him to say, "You make a call now to see the doctor."

"Clarence, you have what we call a heart murmur," Dr. Woods announced. "You can be born with something like that, or even a bad fever can cause it."

"That's what the Army told me. You know I had scarlet fever when I was a kid, Doc," Clarence said matter-of-factly.

Dr. Woods nodded, looking up from his file, "I'll tell you this, Clarence, you have to slow way down. You can't be working wet plaster. As young and strong as you are, you've got the heart of an old man. You could have an attack any minute. Then again, you could live a long, long time if you take care, beginning now."

"Gee, thanks doc," Clarence said sarcastically. "Now, what am I supposed to do with my life?"

Clarence never shied from a challenge. But this time he had a double dilemma to solve. First, he had to sell his house so Philip could go to school. Second, he had to look for a new job, something not as strenuous as wet plastering, to support the family and keep up on Philip's medical bills. He tried one job as a car haul-away driver, but it didn't turn out as he had hoped. His distributor was "as crooked as a dog's hind leg." Within six months, Clarence had lost his investment in his truck and almost lost his house.

Like Father, Like Son

Like the situation with the car hauling business, the move into Detroit proved to be costly, as well. Clarence had it all thought out. Selling his dream castle on a land contract netted Clarence the sum needed for the down payment on a new, westside suburban home. Interest on the monthly payments would help supplement his income. Clarence paid his money and signed the papers, only to find out later that his new home wouldn't be completed for almost a year. With his down payment money tied up and having to vacate their home, Clarence's cousin, Henry, made his cottage on Lake Huron available to them. In payment, Clarence would work for Henry, who farmed and had a plastering business on the side. The arrangement allowed Clarence to drive into the city now and then to check the progress on their new home.

Throughout these months, Philip's abilities were rapidly developing. One time, just before the family moved to the lake, Philip's native mechanical genius revealed itself while he and his Uncle Leo were playing with his trains. Clarence was away for a week, driving his haul-away. Philip carried a broken train engine over to Leo.

"Fikk it," Philip asked, expecting that, like his Dad, all adult men know how to fix things.

"I don't know how to fix it," replied Leo. "You'll have to wait until your Daddy comes home."

"Wire off!" Philip explained. "Has to be ta-dered on!" he said to his bewildered uncle. "I show you how ta fikk it," the boy offered.

"OK, Phil. You show me," said Leo turning the small engine over in his hands, not knowing where to start.

"See da krew in da moketack? Undo it," the boy directed.

Using a tiny screwdriver, Leo undid the screw in the smokestack. At Philip's direction, Leo turned the engine over, and Philip pointed to two more screws between the drive wheels. With the engine shell off of the chassis, Leo now saw that one of the wires to the motor *was* broken.

Leo soldered the wire. Then, little Philip guided his uncle through the steps to get the shell back onto the chassis, fitting it over the valve gear, and getting both piston rods in place at the same time. Handing the engine back to Philip, Leo watched as his nephew placed the engine on the tracks with great difficulty, then turned on the power. Sure enough! The little engine sped along as good as new.

"Hey, Sis!" Leo called up from the basement. "Come see what your son and I did."

As they watched Phil at play, it was clear to Lorraine and Leo that although Philip was physically handicapped, there were no problems with his thought processes or learning abilities, and that he undoubtedly shared many of the talents and mechanical aptitudes of his father.

Another time, after the family moved to the lake, where the yard was mostly sand with a few patches of grass, Philip played quietly, tapping several sticks in a symmetrical pattern into the sandy soil using a small hammer Clarence had given him. The pattern clearly resembled corner posts of a building, with a large stick in the center, symbolizing the peak of a roof. To the tops of the sticks, Philip had draped string for the beams and the roof line.

When Lorraine went out in the yard to see what Philip was doing, Philip said, "I buil_ _ouse _ike daddy." She could see how the sticks were set in order. She had never seen a child his age do something like this. She immediately got the camera and took a photograph.

After Clarence came home and saw what Philip had built, he was so proud he took Philip out for an ice cream. Predictably, Philip promptly dropped the top scoop of the double dip cone, then couldn't eat the remainder fast enough before the second scoop started to drip all over himself. What began as a small celebration had become a defeating experience.

"The little son-of-a-bitch can't even eat a damned ice cream cone!" Clarence growled, embarrassed in front of the other customers and their children.

After Clarence had the tearful Philip cleaned up and in the car, Clarence suddenly asked, "Hey, Phil, you want to drive Daddy's car?"

Once more the mood had shifted. Immediately, Philip stopped crying. And as he sat on Clarence's lap, Phil steered the car down the road.

At home, Philip said, "Mama I dived da car!"

"He sure *did!*" Clarence confirmed.

But again, within minutes, *something* Philip did would upset Clarence, like scuffling his toes across the floor, or losing his balance and hurting himself as he fell; and Clarence would launch into a rage. Not only did Philip have to learn to walk on the shifting moods at home, but he also felt trapped on a teeter-totter of praise and condemnation, a feeling which would grow beyond his home, his doctors, and the hospital, to the world.

In August of the following year, the Schmucker's new house was still not ready. This meant that Philip would miss Kindergarten. When the builder promised their house for the following spring, Clarence and Lorraine, pregnant with their second child, Michael, had no other option but to ask to move in with Lorraine's mother. After Michael's birth, the builder again failed to have their home ready. By this time, Philip was six years old, so, to satisfy residency requirement, Clarence's parents temporarily took in the family.

Philip Begins School

Clarence enrolled Philip in the special school. At first, because Philip had not attended Kindergarten, the school was reluctant to place him in the First Grade. Without a year of Kindergarten to begin socialization with his peers and to gain the behavioral skills needed in an organized environment, the school argued Philip should be placed in Kindergarten. However, Clarence won the battle, and the school agreed to allow Philip to be placed in the First Grade advisedly. Clarence had no idea he risked further handicapping Philip educationally and socially.

Philip was both excited and frightened. He felt this was supposed to be a good thing, but he had no idea what it meant to "go to school." There were a lot of unknowns: what it was, where it was, how he would get there, what he would do there, who would be there, his list went on. Worse, he didn't know how to write! He felt he'd never learn to control a pencil on paper.

The doorbell rang and Ma let in a big stranger, who picked Philip up with his little satchel of paper and pencils and carried him to a big bus at the curb. Everything about the man, the bus, the other kids, everything frightened him. And when the bus finally pulled up to the school, the building itself reminded him of the hospital and the awful months learning to walk.

The First Grade classroom was full of special children, some like him and others who were different. It was like the hospital, but instead of the gentle nurses, the teacher was yelling at two or three children who were not writing good letters on the blackboard. Like him, they could not write letters, and they were in trouble! Philip started to cry. The woman ignored him for some time, then asked an attendant to take Philip to the Kindergarten classroom. By contrast, the Kindergarten class was quiet. This teacher was reading a story. As teary-eyed Philip was brought in, the teacher stopped and walked over to him.

"Well, well, who do we have here?" she asked the attendant. The attendant replied, "Mr. Philip Schmucker. He started in the First Grade this morning, but he's having difficulty adjusting to school. Miss Duty thought he'd do better in your room, Miss Harms."

"That's fine," Miss Harms said, and took Philip by the hand into the circle of children. "Children, this is Philip," she said, introducing him to the others.

They all reacted warmly to him. Miss Harms sat Philip between Michael, who had Cerebral Palsy, and Jackie, a redheaded girl who also had Cerebral Palsy. Returning to her chair, she resumed reading the story. Philip settled in, captivated by the story and the group. He developed special friendships over the years with both Michael and Jackie. In fact, Jackie lived in Clarence's parents' neighborhood, and eventually became Philip's first love.

Just before Philip was dropped off by the bus after school, the school office called to explain what had transpired: how frightened Philip was in the First Grade, and how well he settled into Miss Harms' Kindergarten class. Lorraine listened and consented to the school's recommendation, then thanked them for calling.

Realizing the inevitable, Lorraine waited until Clarence was relaxed on the front porch with the evening paper and his bottle of beer, before she brought up the subject of Philip's first day at school.

"Honey, I have something to tell you about Philip's school."

"*Now* what did he do?" he barked, crushing the paper in his lap as he looked up at her.

"The school placed him back in Kindergarten. They feel he needs Kindergarten to adjust to being in school."

"Puts him a *year* behind all the kids his age! Isn't that great! That damn builder sure screwed up my life!" With that, Clarence shook out his paper and continued to read. There would be nothing more to discuss that evening.

One month after Philip started school, at long last the Clarence Schmucker family moved out of Grandma's and into their own new house. Although Clarence continued to have problems with the builder concerning details throughout the house, this fall was a happy time for them. Clarence and Lorraine finally had a place they could call home.

After four moves in nearly two years, Philip asked Clarence, "Is it for real, Dad?"

Clarence answered, "Forever and ever."

Philip was especially happy because he and his brother had their own room. What's more, Daddy promised to build a table in the basement for his trains.

PHIL'S FIRST STORY

One day Miss Harms announced a special project to the class. She asked the children to draw a picture of who they wanted to be when they grew up. Instead of plain drawing paper, she handed out lined writing paper. For all but one of the children, the lines meant nothing to them as they busily sketched. Philip, however, felt immediately inspired. Miss Harms went around the room checking on the children's drawings, and was surprised that Philip wasn't drawing one of his usual pictures of a locomotive. In fact, he hadn't made a picture at all. Rather, he was making, little marks and scribbles within the lines.

"Philip, what are you drawing?"

Philip looked up at her and grinned from ear to ear, "I _on't traw, _oday. I wite a _tory."

"You are writing a story?" she repeated.

"Uh, huh." Philip beamed.

She lightly chided him for not following the assignment, but allowed Philip to continue his work. She could not hear the approaching train that

Philip heard, carrying with it his inner need to express his ideas, his feelings, his being.

Philip proudly took his story home to show his mother. "_ook, Ma. I wite a _tory _oday." Lorraine complemented him on the scribbles and scratches she saw, but had even less of an idea than Miss Harms what Philip was really trying to express.

The following August, on a recommendation from several acquaintances, including his brother-in-law, Adolph, Clarence applied for a delivery "swing man" job at the Koepplinger bakery. He had truck driving experience, and recommendations from his friends who also worked there had gotten to Mr. Koepplinger.

When Clarence went in to apply, it was as if Mr. K. was ready for him. Clarence was hired on the spot to drive for any delivery route driver who calls in sick. As the bakery grew, and as Clarence's organizational and people skills became known to Mr. K., Clarence's career expanded as well, from "swing man" to route driver to highway supervisor, handling deliveries out of state. When necessary, Clarence himself would drive all night, sometimes taking Philip with him on the road. Soon, other bakeries wanted to hire Clarence, and Mr. K. knew this. So, when he was about to expand his plant once again, Clarence was promoted to maintenance supervisor.

Mr. K. rolled out the prints of his expansion plans for Clarence. "I want to have a maintenance department that can fix anything that breaks down right on the premises. Can you do that for me?"

"You bet, Mr. K.!"

For Clarence it was Christmas morning. Looking at the plans was like being a kid who could take his pick from a catalog full of toys. "Best of all," he thought, "as head of maintenance I'll have no boss except Mr. K., himself!" Clarence's loyalty was highly valued by Mr. Koepplinger, who continued to reward him with increasing levels of trust and responsibility, benefits a man like Mr. K. would have reserved for his own son, the son he never had.

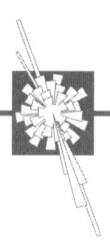

At a simultaneous moment in the Eternal Now, Patricia, God's secretary, enters the Control Center unannounced.

"Sorry, Sir. I left my..."

"Fine report, Patricia," God says, pausing to lift His eyes from the page to compliment her write-up on the soul named Philip.

"Thank you, Sir."

"I know how difficult it is for you to resist editorial comments. Some feel I have the same problem."

"Good Heaven, Sir! You're entitled, after all."

"That's one of the hard things about being Me. I set the rules, and I have to follow them, as well. Not taking someone's inventory is one of My better rules. Never *did* ask Moses how he *missed* that one."

"That's not *all* he missed," Patricia mumbled aloud.

"And speaking of inventories," God went on, gently chiding Patricia by His tone, as well as a look out of the corner of His eye, "Now that little Philip is capable of speaking for himself, I'd like to gain more insight by reviewing the transcriptions of his personal tapes."

"Very good, Sir."

"I know they're all angels in Tape Transcription, but that should save them and you a couple of eternities."

"And the same with the tapes from his soulmate?" asked Patricia.

"Good thinking. Yes, as a matter of fact. Since they're contemporaries on Earth." "Anything else, Sir?"

"Not right now, Patricia. With everything going according to plan, I may just take a break. Hold my calls, will you."

"Yes, Sir."

As God swings around in His overstuffed white leather chair to lose Himself within His universe, Patricia makes an effort to leave the Control Room quietly.

Elsewhere in Heaven, the Tape Transcription Department is changing gears to provide God with the first-person narratives He requested.

As God dreams His favorite recurring dream, Day One of the Old Testament creation story, the moment All Love bursts from His abundance into time and space, Philip Schmucker is beginning the Fourth Grade. His journey well-begun, the complexities of God's wisdom intensify.

you? a writer?

From Kindergarten on, speaking and writing to express myself became terrible obstacles. The teachers in my special school were normally prepared primary and secondary teachers, dedicated to teach "handicapped" kids what they could. They had no idea how to gauge my learning deficits from those of my class mates, who suffered mongolism, hydrocephalism, hemophilia, polio, and other physically debilitating handicaps. As a result, subtle and not-so-subtle messages I received in school haunted me, causing me to doubt my innermost voices.

It may be hard to visualize how someone could be shamed among peers who lived the constant humiliation of severe birth defects, but some staff either did not recognize the issue or were clever in their use of judgment as a weapon of control.

Imagine our class assigned to write an essay in longhand about what we wanted to be when we grew up. Some could write and be read, but I could not. This was an exercise in self-torture that we and our parents suffered for us, dreaming the impossible dream. I wrote in slow painful pencil scratches that I wanted to be a writer. After the teacher corrected our papers, she read each of our essays aloud, with comment.

"Philip, I *think* you say here you want to be a writer. I'm not sure. Your handwriting cannot be read and your spelling is terrible. Writers not only have to write legibly, they have to spell correctly. Because you are unable to do either, I must give you a failing grade. I can't see how you could *ever* be a writer!"

She also failed me in handwriting for the semester. When my Daddy saw that "F" on my report card, he went through the roof about the teacher, who had no business judging the quality of my handwriting. I never again received an "F" in handwriting.

Daddy was right to criticize the teacher. More importantly, his common sense and love helped remove the roadblocks that handwriting and spelling were for me in the development of my writing skills. Even so, it would be many years before I would finally learn I was dyslexic: so much for spelling!

I persisted with my dream to be a writer, in spite of my teachers and the disbelief of my family. In fact, the Christmas after my "F" in handwriting, I asked Santa for a typewriter. I don't know why I trusted Santa to deliver. He never had in the past. Not that he was incompetent, just that he consistently delivered something similar, never *exactly* what I asked for. That Christmas, Santa did it again. He brought a toy typewriter instead of a real one.

I tried to use the toy to type my school work, but it didn't produce the quality I needed. After Daddy realized my practical need and saw my frustration, he actually bought a used typewriter for me. But I didn't have the strength in my fingers nor the physical control to accurately strike the keys.

A year later, IBM offered reconditioned trade-in equipment to the school. Those of us who were judged capable of learning typing skills were given some training and placed on a waiting list. It was six months when I came home from school to find my new typewriter on the dining room table! I dove right in, and typed: P H I L I P   S C H M U C K E R. Something didn't look right. All of the letters looked like capitals. I knew I had only pressed the Shift key for the P and the S, but the lower case letters were capitals, too, only a bit smaller!

When I pointed this out to my mother, she said, "Oh, Philip, it's all right. It's better than nothing. You are never satisfied with anything, are you?"

Disheartened, but not defeated, I accepted the machine the way it was and typed my English assignment. When Daddy came home from work, Mama explained the problem to him. On his way to the fridge for his first evening beer, he grumbled to himself, "The little bastard is never, ever satisfied, is he?"

The next day in English class, I knew I'd get an "A." I proudly exchanged my paper with Donna, who always got "A's," to read and grade. I didn't have any corrections on Donna's paper, and gave her an "A." When she handed back my paper, I was flabbergasted! She had marked everything wrong!

I took my paper up to Mrs. Vorhees and complained, "_ook aw my _apitals are in a'right p_aces!"

Mrs. Vorhees studied the paper and said, "Yes, you are right." She corrected all the marks Donna had made and changed Donna's "F" to a "B." Not the "A" I had expected.

Late that afternoon, Mrs. Vorhees called my house to explain the problem to my mother. "Mrs. Schmucker, there is a problem with the typeface on Philip's typewriter. Other students can't tell the difference between the capitals and the other letters. We think it would be best for Philip to get another typewriter."

Mama agreed to have the typewriter picked up by the program coordinator. Back on the waiting list, it was another six months before I could resume the pursuit of my dream to be a writer.

The Iron, The Teeth, And The Train

Three other related incidents are rooted in my memory to my shame for simply being me. The three happen to begin with Daddy's control over exactly how he thought things should be in his house. It may seem silly that he dictated where my mother should do her ironing, but he did. Daddy thought Mama should iron in the kitchen, like his mother. Mama preferred to iron in front of the bay window in the dining room, from where she could watch Michael and me play outside, or from where she could see into both the living room and the kitchen, when we played inside.

When Daddy came home unexpectedly one day and found Mama ironing in the dining room, he yelled, "Lorraine! How many damn times do I have to tell you to iron in the kitchen!"

"But Honey, I can keep an eye on what the kids are doing and iron at the same time," she argued.

Soon after, on a damp fall morning, the school bus attendant knocked on our door to wake the family. For some reason, our entire family had overslept. The bus went on to school without me. Dad couldn't spare the time to drive me, so I stayed home and played with Michael.

Later that morning, Mama, pregnant with my sister Linda, ironed in the kitchen, while Michael and I amused ourselves in the living room. Somewhere in the action, he picked up a souvenir paper weight and heaved it at my face. He was too fast for me. Mama heard me scream and ran from the kitchen to find me lying on the couch, my two adult top front teeth knocked loose in my open mouth, blood running down my chin. Two-year-old Michael stood there smiling, "I do-ed that!"

Ma and a neighbor, Dorothy Preston, rushed me to a local dentist, who cleaned the wound, concluding, "I'm very sorry, Mrs. Schmucker, but there is absolutely nothing more that can be done for Philip at this point. Maybe when he's fourteen."

Mama cried long after Daddy came home from work, as he raged on about who's fault it was and what this would cost him. The hell was indescribable that night, but it ended long before the pain loosened its grip on me enough to allow me to sleep.

From that day on, Mama ironed in the dining room. And this seven-year-old little boy with Cerebral Palsy, who constantly gagged on his own drool, began a long and painful dental restoration process with two root canals at the hands of a nearly retired and very impatient old dentist.

I know I'm not the only kid in the world to ever have two front teeth knocked out by his brother, but a lot of what went on in the house continuously divided me from Michael and my two sisters Linda and Laurie. From little on, he was jealous and resentful, always on the short end for attention from Daddy. What attention he *did* get, he got for causing trouble, which included breaking my toys.

By this time, Daddy had started to build the train table he promised me. But as I watched him work on it, if he caught me drooling, walking on my toes, or holding my hands out like "wings," he'd angrily stop work and leave me alone in the basement. In no time, the table was built, the track layout nailed in place and wired up. His artistry with wet plaster was displayed in lifelike mountains, railway tunnels and sloping valleys.

Like Daddy told me, I was very careful not to run the train too fast, because it might jump the track, fall on the floor, and break. One Saturday, as Michael played in one corner of the basement, I ran my train. Suddenly, Michael reached up to the table and picked the engine off the tracks, thinking he'd roll it along on the concrete floor. I simply couldn't react in time. And he knew I'd be angry. But in his selfish glee, he lost his grip, and the "pot metal" vintage engine shattered like glass against the cement. He stood in the engine rubble laughing, "I do-ed that!"

Later that afternoon, when Daddy came home, all hell broke loose. Not only was the engine broken beyond repair, but worse yet, Daddy growled: "You'll just have to ask Santa Claus for another engine. I sure can't afford to replace it now."

This was terrible. Santa Claus never delivered what was asked. But as Christmas came around, I decided to trust Santa one more time, and I put in my specifications.

That Christmas, I learned something new about Santa. He sometimes brought *nothing*. It would be another year and I would be ten before Santa delivered a new toy train to my house. That following Christmas morning, a new steam engine and three cars were under the tree!

I plugged the transformer into the wall and made the engine go, but the cars didn't follow. I looked at the engine and discovered that the coupler was broken! In fact, this was not the train set I had specified! The engine didn't smoke, and none of the three cars was a boxcar, my favorite! Santa delivered a broken toy to a broken boy. This was the Christmas I gave up on Santa Claus.

Teenager

Suddenly, thirteen! I hardly fit the teen image. My body was bigger, but I was still bent at the knees, hips and back, so that I didn't look any taller. I still tiptoed with my hands and elbows folded awkwardly: my "wings." I was thirteen, but I was not the cliche misty-eyed type with dreams and ambitions. I hadn't learned to write legibly or speak intelligibly. Worse yet, I still drooled, often gagging on my saliva. I lived so intensely in the present, I gave little thought to my purpose or my life goals.

There *was* a voice within that surfaced through the daily negative clutter of family, doctors, school, and school mates. and with which I continue to wrestle to this day. And there was a second, a happy "little kid" voice, which came through on two occasions in my teen years.

My Daddy's stepfather, Grandpa Hennicken, told me wide-eyed, "Philip, there be a million dollars out there with your name on it!"

Excited, I asked, "Pa, where is it?"

"Well, it's there!" sweeping his arm in the air. "All you have to do is to find a way to make it!" he said, knowingly. He really believed that for me. He believed that about Daddy. About America. That idea kept me going.

Another time the "little" voice came through was during a conversation with my mother. I'm sure I was always asking her why God made me with Cerebral Palsy. I knew it was a painful question for me to ask. But her stock answer never made an impression until I was thirteen. For some strange reason, "Honey, God has a purpose for making you this way, and someday we will know what it is" made sense to this teenager.

One area that didn't make sense about being a teenager included all of the physical changes puberty was producing in my body. No one told me what would happen. And, I guess no one warned Kathy Bennett, the little red head who sat behind me in class. She developed a full blown case of puppy love for me. I thought I was unlovable. What's more, she must have said something to her friends, because soon everybody acted like there was something going on between us. I didn't have a clue. I had "feelings" and "stirrings," but I didn't know what they were.

Kathy got my address and sent me a letter. A "love letter," my classmate Michael called it. She wrote, "I love you dearly and want to marry you. I will wait for you, forever!"

I hardly knew Kathy. She was new and ended up leaving my school after that year. I actually preferred playing with the other little redhead, Jackie, who I had known since Kindergarten. Of course, Mama found her letter and was appalled. She called the school, demanded the two of us be separated and that she be given Kathy's home telephone number. I didn't know what to make of the whole thing. And I didn't much care, until Ma made me sit there when she made the call to Kathy's mother.

"Mrs. Bennett? This is Mrs. Schmucker. Your daughter Kathy is in my son Philip's class. I am calling about a letter your daughter sent to Philip." She read the entire letter over the telephone, then added, "I think it is a disgrace for children to act this way, sending love letters!"

Now, the whole world knew what was in the letter! I was totally humiliated. I decided that if I ever had feelings about a girl, I'd keep them to myself. And now that my mother had made me "untouchable," it wasn't a big step in my state of mind to go to "unlovable," as school mates, and, soon after that, my only neighborhood playmate temporarily shunned me.

Robert Dubkowski lived across the street. Other kids on the block never would play with me. Only Robert. One day after school, after I knocked on his door, he told me, "I can't play today." Same thing the next day. The next. And the next. I turned home with tears in my eyes. I knew I was being rejected, and why.

"Mama, Robert don't want to play with me anymore."

Mama immediately called Robert's mother on the phone. "Mrs. Dubkowski, this is Lorraine Schmucker, Philip's mother. Is there some reason why Robert won't play with Philip? Philip thinks the world of Robert and is sad Robert can't play with him."

Mrs. Dubkowski didn't hold anything back. "If Philip got hurt, you would hold me and my husband responsible. We don't want to be sued."

Without pause Mama said, "Let me tell you this. I know my son is handicapped. I know he has a very good chance of getting hurt when he is outside playing, a fact of life we have to live with everyday. If he should get hurt, there will be no one to blame. Now, thanks to you, there is more pain for Philip because he can't play with Robert than if he had been hurt."

A few days later, Robert came back across the street to play, but it didn't last, as the other boys in the block would say, "Hey, Robert, wanna play baseball?" Off he'd go, leaving me to play alone. Mama kept telling me everything would be OK when I grew up. The "little kid" inside wanted to believe her, but there were too many other signs that fed that other angry voice that told me nothing would change.

SCOUTING

Daddy and I continued to act out our intense day-to-day seesaw relationship. His frustrations, which often boiled over into anger, fed by my inherent weaknesses, teased by my talents and abilities, were dashed time and again by a rebellious laziness in me that was too ready to give it all up. Worse yet, I idolized him, as did everyone else, frustrating him all the more, as he came to accept that I'd never be fixed, made totally whole, and be the perfect son he'd dreamed of for himself. Mama saw both sides and prayed hard to keep Daddy and me sane through these years.

Scouting was Mama's miracle! Without a lot of fanfare, Daddy took me to our church one night for a Scout meeting. It must have been prearranged, because the assistant scoutmaster met me at the door, then called the troop to attention and announced my arrival and new nickname, "Gentlemen, allow me to introduce you to Cannonball!"

He had a unique nickname for all fifty of us! Like "Solid Gold Joe," or "Sparkle Like Diamonds." Our nicknames fit our personality or our interests. Mine was trains, so "Cannonball" it was. I was assigned to the Beaver Patrol.

The scoutmasters were former WWII sergeants, which helped make Troop 527 a crackerjack outfit, the best in the city.

I loved being a boy scout. I couldn't wait for each Monday night meeting. Scouting allowed me to express all of my talents. I learned to tie all of the knots, read maps, render first aid, even cook. I learned how to find my way in the woods without a compass, using only nature signs. I especially loved lashing logs together with ropes. Whatever it was, I was the fastest-learning scout in the troop.

Daddy and I both made an impression on the troop. Daddy eventually became a committeeman. He built modular storage lockers for each patrol to store their camping gear. They contained drawers, secret compartments and came apart to make tables. No other troop in the country had these! Daddy even convinced Mr. Koepplinger to donate the use of a truck so our troop could transport all of our new equipment.

Everyone thought Daddy was the greatest thing to happen to Troop 527. For me, the pressure to perform to Daddy's higher standards was almost too much to bear. He even had Dr. Walsh fit me with leg braces after being free of them since I was five, because he thought I wasn't walking right. One night, I fell and the braces tore a hole in the pants of my new uniform.

On the short ride home in the car, he yelled, "You dumb bastard! Did you have to fall and tear a hole in your damn new uniform? Now, I have to go and spend more of my damn hard-earned money to buy you new pants so you won't embarrass me in front of everybody!"

Petrified with fear, my enthusiasm and excitement from the evening had totally vanished.

Then, there were the great times at the weekend District Meets, when all of the troops would meet at a local campground. The main event would be the building of signal towers, from which the troops would signal back and forth with flags. The towers were constructed of heavy logs lashed with the same techniques we learned in our weekly meetings. I knew better than most just what to do, but I wasn't allowed to help. I'd keep asking and get back, "You can't!"

The following week, I decided I'd build my own tower. I bought wooden dowels at my favorite hobby shop. Mama cut them to scale, and I lashed them together with string. At the next meeting, I received a lot of praise for my achievement. My tower was the center of attraction at our next Court of Honor.

Each summer, my troop conducted an outing on Mackinac Island in northern Michigan with all the scouts and our dads. Some families made it their vacation, so some Moms, including mine, came along, too. Although there was some tension between Mama and Daddy at the time, it helped take the edge off between me and Daddy to have Mama there.

Camping means hiking. And there was no way I could hike with the troop. So, Daddy worked for two months before the trip building me a custom-fitted sulky in the bakery machine shop. I still marvel at the way Daddy could make something without plans from metal strap and plate, spot weld, then finish off the details, as if by instinct.

I'd go with him to the bakery maintenance department, not only to watch, but to be there so he could measure my body. He'd always have one eye on me. And if he saw me not walking right, not standing right, or drooling on myself, or slurring, he'd quit working on the sulky and work on something else, while making me walking up and down the length of the building.

"You see now how you can walk! You think I *like* doing this to you?" He'd have me practice walking all night if it wasn't for Mama.

The sulky created other problems at home. Daddy scavenged parts that he couldn't fabricate from the bicycles of my brother, Michael, and my two little sisters, Linda and Laurie. They didn't appreciate being without their bicycles from May until the end of July. Phil, Daddy and Mama were going off on a camping trip, leaving them at Grandma's without their bicycles.

The week on Mackinac Island was great fun for me. My fellow scouts actually argued who would pull me in the sulky. By the end of the week, the whole island knew about Troop 527 marching down Main Street with me in my sulky.

The culmination of the weekend was a closing ceremony called "Burying The Hatchet." As we returned from the island on the ferry, a ceremonial hatchet was passed, and on it each of us placed any bad feelings we had from the trip. This year, the ceremony was even more elaborate, including a parade around the boat, accompanied by the ferry's brass band. I was specially designated to lead the parade and toss the hatchet overboard midway from the island to the mainland.

I didn't know what it was at the time, but Daddy was furious about *something*. Perhaps it was something between him and Mama. Perhaps it was the way I held the hatchet, or I may have drooled. During the march around the boat, his anger grew to where it was evident to everyone. By the time we reached the stern, although I was shaking with fear, I didn't let it deter me. I gave a giant heave to the hatchet, sailing it far out into the wake of the ferry to the cheers of the entire shipboard crowd.

He's A Good Doctor

Late that next spring, on an early June morning, Daddy pulled into the bakery parking lot next to his maintenance building as the night shift was walking to their cars. He quickly picked up right where he had left off the night before, fabricating a sesame seed sprinkling machine from scratch to save Karl Koepplinger $1,500.

Within minutes, Karl Koepplinger, heavy set and in his early sixties, pulled his black Lincoln up to the open overhead door and walked to where Daddy was working. Daddy was so engrossed in his machining that he didn't notice Karl had walked in.

"Clarence, I want to talk to you."

Showing the same stubborn indifference he showed that day when Mama announced she was pregnant with me, Daddy continued to drill a hole in a piece of steel. Karl wouldn't be ignored. He stepped to the electric control panel and shut off the power to the drill press.

"What do you want?" Daddy asked brusquely.

"Clarence, I want to talk to you," Mr. K. firmly repeated. "I have been letting you get away with murder here, Clarence, running this place night and day by yourself. Sometimes I wonder if I own this bakery or you!"

"So?"

"You are forcing me to watch you work yourself to death! You are too valuable to me and to your family for me to sit back and let you work like this, especially, when I know you're not well. I have arranged for you to see a very good doctor this afternoon, who is a friend of mine. You have a two o'clock appointment for a complete checkup. I want you to go home now and rest up for it."

"I've got to finish this sesame seed sprinkler!"

"Damn this machine! You are more important to me and your family than a silly seed sprinkler! Can't you see that, man?"

A doctor hadn't examined Daddy since he had been warned many years before by the family doctor to give up the wet plastering trade. Daddy and Mama said nothing as they waited to be led into an examining room. Soon the receptionist invited them in.

"Mr. Shoemaker, you may come in, now, please."

"The name is Schmucker, not Shoemaker," Daddy retorted. "How the hell do you get Shoemaker from S-C-H-M-U-C-K-E-R?"

Mama nudged him.

The receptionist blushed. "Oh, yes, Schmucker. Sorry."

Just then, a handsome, middle-aged man joined them. The receptionist handed Daddy's file to the man and left.

"Good afternoon Lorraine, Clarence, I'm Dr. Ryan."

Mama and Daddy never heard a doctor use their first names before.

"Karl told me a lot about you, including all of the great things you are doing for his bakery. He really cares about you. So, let's see if I can help you feel better."

After nearly twenty years of worry that she might lose Daddy to a heart attack, Mama sat quietly, hanging onto every syllable of the doctor's findings.

"Clarence, you have a serious heart condition we call, Congenital Heart Failure. To make matters worse, you are overweight and overworking yourself at the bakery. You are going to have to slow down at work and take off about fifty pounds. When you're rested in a few weeks, we'll run some tests to see if you qualify for a new surgery, where we graft strong veins from your legs to replace the weakened veins around your heart."

"But will he have a heart attack?" Lorraine anxiously blurted out.

"No, nothing like that, Lorraine. His heart will simply pump more slowly until it stops, unless something is done now to slow him down at work, reduce his anxiety, lose weight, and the combination of surgery and medicines to keep Clarence's heart going strong. I don't want any more talk or worry about heart attacks, OK?"

It was as if a terrible weight had been lifted from her own heart. For the first time in her married life, Mama was able to live without the fear of Daddy having a heart attack.

Dr. Ryan saw Daddy once a week. His diet was difficult, especially having to cut down on his beer. Worst of all was cutting back at work. Daddy's whole adult life was work. His obsessions, like paying off the mortgage early, or getting me to walk and talk normally, only drove him instead to work harder and longer. Looking back, they seemed to point to a deep feeling within himself that he had a limited time to set everything in order. Why else would he say, "Look at me dying and I can't get you to walk and talk right!"?

Fix Philip

I didn't realize what he was feeling. But the more he pushed, the more repressed, shamed and useless I felt. My uncontrollable drooling was the subject of our next visit with Dr. Walsh.

"I do have an idea, Mr. Schmucker, which may help solve the problem, but as I said before, when Philip reaches the age where he cares about the way he looks, he will stop the drooling and walk and talk right," Dr. Walsh said to reassure Daddy.

"I can't wait that long!" Daddy snapped back.

A few days later, I went to the clinic at my school for this new therapy to correct my drooling. I knew what was coming. Miss Stock, the therapist who had become adept at frightening me since early childhood, proceeded to wind an ace bandage under my chin and around the top of my head that locked my jaws shut.

"Philip, we are going to put a stop to your drooling one way or another."

Suddenly, I thought I was going to suffocate. Petrified, I tried to communicate that to her, but she didn't seem to care.

"Not talking for a while will do you some good, Philip. No one can understand you, anyway."

Then, she placed a football helmet on my head to anchor the bandage. When I was sent back to class like this, I found my desk had been moved to the back of the room and faced the wall. A set of three mirrors, that I had watched my Daddy proudly hinge together, had been set up on my desk, which forced me to watch myself drool.

Next, the knees. The muscles and tendons had to be straightened out. At home, as I laid face down on the bed, Mama strapped twenty-pound weights to my ankles. The pain was incredible. And after a few sessions, something went wrong and my knee caps were permanently damaged. I required a wheelchair for several weeks, until the pain subsided. After that I used crutches to get around.

All this time my grades were failing and Daddy and Mama were wondering why. I was wondering why I was being tortured. Why was I being singled out, when my classmates, Michael and Jackie both drooled? No one had any answers for me, except something within that said there *had* to be a reason, a purpose, and that I would understand, *someday*.

Lutheran High School

There was only one alternative to the two city high schools, that took students with disabilities, Lutheran High School. Mama made an appointment to meet with Mr. Olschlager, the admissions counselor. It was a familiar experience for Mama. One more moment that gave her hope that everything would work out for the best and that Philip would be happy. In contrast, I was not comfortable in the little hot and humid church office. For me, it was just another waiting room, another day of judgment, another institution full of strangers my parents would blindly entrust me to.

Mr. Olschlager, a heavy-set man came out of his office, soaked with perspiration, his shirt tail hanging out over his belt, his collar unbuttoned and his necktie yanked down at a careless angle. As he thumbed through a file folder containing information Mama had given him over the phone, he asked me a lot of questions I had no idea how to answer.

"What courses do you want to take, Philip?"

"I think I want to take college prep," I blurted out.

"Do you think you will be able to do the school work? You know, high school will be much harder than grade school."

After a few minutes, he made some notes in the file, then summed up his thoughts.

"Mrs. Schmucker, I don't think your son will be able to handle the challenges he will face here at Lutheran High West. I'm sorry."

When I arrived home, I went up to my room and cried. Mama knew it would do no good to call Daddy. In tears, she called our pastor.

"Pastor Jesse, Philip and I just got back from Lutheran High West. They won't take Philip. I don't know what to do."

In his usual soothing, reassuring voice, Pastor Jesse said, "Let me take care of it, Lorraine. Don't worry anymore. Everything will be all right. Philip will go to Lutheran High West."

The next afternoon, Mr. Olschlager called to arrange for my enrollment at Lutheran High West. Pastor Jesse had fulfilled his promise with the threat to withhold the financial support of our church if I wasn't accepted. He left no room for debate.

On my first day, Mr. Olschlager again tried to renegotiate. "Philip, we have decided to give you a couple of classes to start and see how you do."

"Nooo!" I shouted. "I can do it all, just like the other kids. I want to be like the other kids." I was very emphatic.

Mr. Olschlager sat way back in his chair, stretched his arms out, and said, "Well, all right, we'll give you a chance to show us what you can do."

All dressed up in my new school clothes, armed with a new briefcase, I knew what I had to do, even if somebody *did* pull strings to get me the opportunity. I was determined to prove myself. But I was so scared on the way that I counted the cross-streets just to take my mind off my fright.

In the school driveway, Mama asked, "Do you have everything?"

"Ya," I said.

"You know where to go?"

"Ya," I said, remembering the piece of paper in my pocket with my schedule and locker number. "German 1."

"Have a good time!" she said, as I opened the heavy door of the Oldsmobile.

I was feeling alone and abandoned, and my mother was wishing me to have a good time? It was 7:50 and my first class started at 8:00. I made my way along the wall to find my locker, which I found less than twenty feet from the entrance and right next to the door of my first class. Taking my new notebook with all the new writing paper in it, I walked into a new chapter of my life. And as the day wore on, I could feel a sense of relaxation and even enjoyment. For the first time in my life, I was in a world without peers with handicaps, and I was being accepted. More than that, I was functioning well.

By 3:00, I was exhausted. I dragged myself and my briefcase full of text books out to the red and white Oldsmobile and climbed in. The next thing I remember is the car turning into our driveway.

"Time to change your clothes and go do homework, honey."

"Ya. OK." I mumbled, groggy from my catnap.

After I had been struggling with my homework for about two hours, wondering about a lot of other things, like, would I ever have time to run my trains, or ride my bike again, Mama called me down for dinner. I could hear Daddy's '38 Ford Coupe rumbling in the driveway. It needed a new muffler but Daddy wouldn't take the time or spend the money to fix it.

The food had to be on the table when Clarence came in the door. It was always a competition to see which one of us, me, Michael, Linda, or Laurie, would get Daddy his beer, paper and slippers. If they wanted Daddy's time that evening, those were the price of admission. After he drank his first beer of the evening, we would take our places. The food was not as hot as it was when he walked through the door, but that was the way he wanted things to be done.

I had just taken my first bite of food, when Daddy asked me how my first day went at Lutheran High West. I tried to respond, "All right," but I choked on the food and coughed some out onto the table. All hell broke out!

"You little bastard! How many damn times do I have to tell you not to cough with food in your mouth! Did you do that in school? If you do, those kids won't want to have a damn thing to do with you!"

"Honey leave him alone, let him eat," Mama interrupted. "You know it's the Cerebral Palsy that makes him cough."

"Fine! Let him go. Remember what the doctor said about the kid being able to control the coughing when he learns to give a damn."

Suddenly, Daddy's rage erupted and the bottle of catsup smashed a hole in the kitchen door. With that, he stood up and tossed the entire kitchen table over, sending food and dishes every which way.

"There! See what you made me do, you little bastard! You keep making me get mad like this, making these messes, and some day you're going to kill me!"

Mama cried, "Honey you shouldn't blame *him*. You know perfectly well it's your own temper that caused this mess!"

As he left the house, he slammed the door with a force that shook the windows.

We helped Mama salvage what she could to eat, then went to our rooms, while she cleaned up the mess.

I was in bed, when Daddy came home around 11:00. Mama and Daddy said nothing. I laid awake for hours unable to sleep, frightened about school and Daddy, feeling everyone would be better off if I were dead.

The next evening, Daddy couldn't stop teasing me at the table about the hole in the kitchen door.

"Gee, that's a nice hole you put in the door, Philip."

We were all quivering in our chairs, poking at our food.

Just as suddenly as his anger came, it went. The entire mood at the supper table changed. Then, later in the evening, after Daddy had another beer and read the evening paper, he called up to me, "Philip, ya want to go to the hardware store with me?"

I knew what he wanted to do: buy what he needed to fix the hole in the kitchen door. I sensed a change in his voice, and I thought it was safe. Besides, I always jumped at the chance to go somewhere with Daddy. So, off we went to stroll the aisles of our neighborhood hardware together. Daddy was like a god to me. I watched him gather the things he needed to rebuild his universe.

But my god came crashing down soon after he started talking with the clerk.

"Philip and I are here to buy the things we need to fix the hole he put in the door last night."

My shame was crushing. I stood at the checkout wanting to escape, wishing I were dead. Long after the hole was repaired, Daddy perpetuated this little "joke" to all who wanted to see the fantastic job he did fixing the hole I put in the door, including the duplication of the birch grain. By contrast, sometime later, after Mama threw her set of keys at his head, scarring a cabinet door over the stove, did he rush to repair it, as well?

"You fix it!" he protested, and it remained un-mended.

daddy is dying

Toward the end of my sophomore year, although I managed to keep up with my studies, I was losing interest in school. In scouts, I was one merit badge away from star scout. But there, too, lack of interest and low self-esteem dragged me down. Our troop was the best in the state, thanks to Daddy's enthusiasm, not mine.

At the same time, Daddy's health was deteriorating rapidly. Against Dr. Ryan's advice, finishing the sesame seed sprinkling machine remained an obsession to the exclusion of managing the other aspects of the maintenance department. All of that he left by default to his assistant, Don Makemson. Daddy worked day and night, pushing himself relentlessly, rather than delegate.

The end of June can produce some of the nicest weather of the season. One late June Monday morning that dawned bright and clear, Daddy was already hours into his day working on the sesame seed sprinkler, when Don came into work at 8:00. The warm breeze refreshed the building from one end to the other. Don had learned, like Mama and me, how to merge into Daddy's intense concentration without interrupting. In some ways, Don was the son neither I nor Michael would ever be. Lost in their work, they were both startled by the voice of Karl Koepplinger.

"Good morning, gentlemen. How's the machine comin' along, Clarence?"

Daddy turned to speak, but he couldn't catch his breath. It took Daddy several painful minutes to recover. Don assured Karl there was no emergency, then excused himself to give Karl some time alone with Daddy, who had simply returned to his work on the machine after catching his breath.

"Clarence, how many times have I told you not to work so hard. I pay you a salary for 40 hours. That's all the time I expect you to work. I don't want to see you here after 5 p.m."

Exasperated, Daddy yelled at Karl, "All right! *You* finish the damn thing!" He threw his tools down emphasizing his point and walked over to his desk and poured a cup of coffee from his thermos. Flopping into his squeaky swivel chair, he struggled for his breath.

Karl followed, "You know, Dr. Ryan still had hopes you'd be a good candidate for that new bypass surgery."

"Yeah? Well, who in hell is going to pay for it?"

"I will!" Karl shouted without missing a beat. He so rarely shouted that he surprised himself. Then, in a calmer tone, he asked, "When do you see Dr. Ryan next?"

"Wednesday. But I need a couple more weeks to finish the machine!"

"The *hell* you do! We've been all through this! Don will finish the machine. I have as much faith in him as you."

Karl meant what he said, but he couldn't have thought Daddy would be so hurt. The instant Daddy's face fell, Karl wished he had never said those words. As Karl continued to speak, Daddy focused on the sound of the breeze kicking up at the other end of the building, where a small dust devil was whipping up some dirt and grass clippings and toying with them in the air. The sudden chug of the air compressor motor broke the grip of Daddy's reverie.

Daddy said nothing as Don came back into the building and Karl asked, "Don, do you think you could finish the machine?"

Not realizing how he was compounding the "injury" and, perhaps, feeling emboldened to speak of his skills to Karl, Don said, "Sure, no problem. I know this thing as good as Clarence. I'll have it working in about a week."

"Clarence, I'm putting you on leave with full salary for the duration. You can't very well argue with that, can you?"

"Mr. ..."

"That's final!" insisted Karl. "I want you out of here and resting at home within the hour. Am I making myself clear?"

At that, Karl left to walk to his office. Don had already walked out of the other end of the building. The compressor motor stopped. Daddy finished the last sip of cold coffee, wiped out his cup, replaced it on his thermos, and without a look back, walked out into the sunlit parking lot to where his prized '38 Ford Coupe patiently awaited him, and was gone.

THE HOSPITAL STAY

During Daddy's next appointment, Dr. Ryan made arrangements for Daddy to be admitted to Ford Hospital for tests. Because bypass surgery was in its infancy, Daddy's eligibility for the procedure had to be determined by a myriad of medical data. Nothing about the hospital or the tests was pleasant for Daddy. He was a man of action.

Between tests, Mama told me Daddy would sit on the edge of his bed and either stare at the bustling traffic on the freeway five stories below, or he'd brag to the attending nurses about his son, Philip, who, despite CP, was in a regular high school, active in the Boy Scouts, and full of energies and talents just like his Dad. "Boy, Philip is the greatest!"

The next Thursday, the medical chief of surgery, Dr. Ryan, and Karl Koepplinger, all came in to see him. The looks on their faces, even the expression of the nurse as she left the room and closed the door, gave Daddy a sinking feeling. As he laid back, the three men circled his bed. Doctor Ryan spoke.

"Clarence, it seems we waited a bit too long to repair your heart valves. I am sorry."

"Oh, God, no," Daddy moaned as he laid there motionless.

Dr. Ryan continued, "But I'm sure we can keep you going for a few more years."

Karl added, "The team also agrees, after you've rested up for a few weeks, and if you continue to take care of yourself, you could even return to the bakery. You'd have to direct Don and the other men to do the actual work, of course."

Just then, Mama walked into the room for her daily visit. Surprised at seeing the three men standing there, she knew immediately what had taken place. The two doctors said good-bye and left the room. Karl stood there at a loss for words.

"Clarence, take care of yourself. I need you. You know the bakery can't run without you," Karl said. "Good-bye, Lorraine," he added, then, left the room.

Daddy told Mama what Dr. Ryan said. Without comment, she took her usual chair in the corner, pulled out her latest crochet project from her tote bag as she had all that week, and continued her vigil.

FINAL DAYS

Mama spent every possible minute in Daddy's presence at the hospital. There seemed to be little else for her to do except to await the inevitable. The doctors wouldn't release Daddy until his medication began working to stabilize his vital signs, but nothing seemed to slow Daddy's decline beginning that Thursday morning. Within eight days, Daddy was dead.

The Thursday before Daddy died, George, a friend of the family, who felt he could never repay Daddy for the things he had done for him, brought the four of us children to see Daddy. When we arrived, Daddy was sitting on the edge of the bed, his legs over the side, his elbows resting on the night stand, his head cradled in his palms. I sat in a chair next to the window. Without warning, Daddy began to scream at me.

"What the hell are you drooling for? All these years and what is likely to be the last time you see me alive, you have to goddamn drool!"

I must have jumped a mile up in shock. And, of course, my drooling only got worse with me in tears. George hurried me out of the room and down the hall to the lounge. Mama and the others sat there without a word, as if nothing had happened. When we returned a short time later, the hush in the room was suffocating. Daddy laid motionless in his bed, staring at the ceiling.

George whispered to Mama, "Guess I'll take the kids home."

"Take the three," replied Mama. "I want Philip to stay."

Mama and I remained well past visiting hours. Daddy was quiet until we began to go. She kissed him good night, and I heard him softly say, "Honey, the machine don't work no more."

Of the car ride home, I remember the empty streets. I remember the blur of the street lights. I remember a long silence.

Then, Mama said, "You know he didn't mean it."

That was that.

Although Mama stopped for a prescription from Dr. Ryan to help us both sleep, Mama sat up most of the night in the overstuffed chair Daddy had just reupholstered, keeping her vigil with a glass of wine and the soothing tick-tock of the cuckoo clock. When the phone rang just before 1 a.m., Mama jolted awake. She lifted the receiver, choked with dread.

"Hello?"

Pastor Jesse did all the talking.

"Pastor Jesse, Lorraine. I am here at Ford. I came back in about 11 p.m. because, when I saw Clarence yesterday, I knew he was about to die."

Mama hadn't breathed.

"Lorraine?"

"Mmmm hmm."

"I want to tell you Clarence and I had a long talk tonight. He told me how much he loves you. How there have been many, many times he couldn't express his love to you and the kids. He told me how he thinks Linda and Laurie are the two most beautiful daughters a man could want. He said Michael is just like him, with a mind of his own. No one is ever going to push him around. And he thinks Philip is really going to make it on his own, someday."

Mama tried to take a long, deep breath without being heard.

"The nurses said that after you left last night, Clarence talked and talked about you and the kids, especially Philip, and the many great things he can do despite his Cerebral Palsy. He talked for a couple of hours. Then, after he was talked out, we hugged each other, and he laid back in his bed and became very still. I called a nurse, who immediately sounded a Code Blue. I left his room, then. And just a little while ago, Lorraine, he died. Lorraine, remember what our Lord said? 'My grace is sufficient unto you.' "

Tears in her eyes, Mama took another deep, but silent breath.

"Good night, Lorraine. I'll call again later today. Everything will work out for the good. God bless."

Mama stayed in the chair, drained of all energy and emotion, and eventually fell asleep. Grandma found her at 5 a.m. and sent her off to bed.

At 8 a.m. that same morning at the Koepplinger Bakery, Daddy's sesame seed sprinkler was installed in the production line, and there it remained without a down shift for the next twenty-five years.

The Funeral

I woke feeling quite groggy from the pill Mama had given me. Already, the July heat and humidity were unbearable. I heard male voices downstairs. Sliding down the steps, I stood up slowly and peeked through a crack in the door to see Mama and my two uncles. Daddy, my hero, the ogre, was gone! No more demands! No more terror! Banished! Dead!

Uncle Les took Linda and Laurie for the day. Uncle Paul took me and Michael to his place. Mama spent the day preparing Daddy's funeral.

Sunday morning, after the usual bustle of breakfast, we were dressed up and rustled into Uncle Les' car to drive to the funeral parlor, as if to bathe ourselves in the horror of the absolute truth. I trembled as I moved toward Daddy's body. I lost my balance and fell. Uncle Les picked me up and carried me the rest of the way. Daddy's cold hands were empty of reassurance.

After the family viewing, the doors were opened to the mourners. They had been gathering before we had arrived. The funeral director had never seen anything like it before. Within another hour, there were so many mourners there was no room for everyone to sit and visit with the family. The director opened the entire facility to our family to accommodate the overflow, until people stood four abreast to view Daddy. At that point, the director called other funeral parlors to borrow chairs, plus additional flags for the following day's motorcade. He also thought to arrange for police help to direct traffic.

Tuesday, the crowd swelled inside the church until it could hold no more. Many had to wait in their cars until the motorcade to the cemetery. The extra vehicle flags were not enough. Later, I heard someone say the funeral director stopped counting cars in the motorcade after seventy-five.

When Mama had asked the Scouts to be Daddy's pallbearers, she had no idea they'd literally make over the proceedings in military fashion, complete with taps at the grave site.

Back home after the cemetery, the neighbors took charge of the wake. Our entire block contributed food and drink for the family and the multitude. Clarence Schmucker had what can best be described as a glorious send-off into eternity.

I HAVE A JOB FOR YOU

Two days after the funeral, Mama had an early morning appointment with Mr. Koepplinger to sign papers for Daddy's Social Security. Karl escorted her into his plush office with all his African trophies hanging on the walls and directed her to an overstuffed couch. He sat behind his huge mahogany desk.

"Lorraine, I think you know how much Clarence meant to me. He was like the son Anna and I could never have. I have decided to help you and the kids in any way I can. First, as you may know, I promised Clarence I'd take care of all the hospital bills. I will also pay the funeral expenses. But since the insurance you will receive from Social Security will not be enough to make ends meet, you will need a job. I will have an opening in September, selling the returned bread in the Stale House. But until you start in the fall, I will continue to pay Clarence's wages, even though I've moved Don Makemson into Clarence's position. Now, what do you think about all of that?"

Mama couldn't find words. Tears of gratitude welled up in her eyes. She began to sob. Karl called in his secretary to comfort Mama. When she was calm again, he continued.

"I admire Philip. I think he will go a long way in life. I always thought, however, Clarence was a bit too demanding on him much of the time. I think Clarence was asking more of Philip than he was capable of delivering. I know Philip is bright. In fact, I wish I could hire *him* for his intelligence."

The money from Karl Koepplinger made those first months a lot easier for Mama. She was able to give us our annual vacation in northern Michigan, which took the edge off our grief. Soon enough, however, September came and it was time for us to return to school and for Mama start her new job. Grandma Zehnder wanted to help, so she closed her home and moved in with us.

Mama hadn't worked since she was a clerk in a five and dime long before she and Daddy were married. At the bakery, she quickly realized this was a backbreaking job. It was selling returned bread, all right. But, first, Mama had to unload the bread from the returning delivery trucks, count the loaves, then stack them in the Stale House. Thirty loaves in a box weighed thirty pounds.

Actually, the Stale House was no stranger to Mama or me. We both had watched Daddy build it. In fact, he would make us wait in the car some evenings while he continued to trowel cement as he laid the slab, and later, when he'd insist on completing a course of bricks before knocking off for lack of light.

No one in the company thought Mama could do the work. Bets were made at the bakery on when she'd quit. She would have bet against herself after that first day, as she dragged herself into the house and crashed on the couch. She didn't move from that spot for much of the evening until Grandma shook her.

"Come on, Lorraine, time to get yourself to bed. You can't sleep here all night!"

Mama didn't know what day it was. She ate leftovers, then drew a hot tub for herself. As she lay soaking in the tub, she yelled out in pain to her mother, "Ma, I am going to do this job if it kills me!"

Grandma went into the bathroom, took one look at Lorraine and said, "By the way you look tonight, I'd say it will."

The next morning, Mama had to force herself to go to work. Tuesday proved to be even more stressful. But the saving grace was her split week schedule. With Wednesdays and Sundays off, she had a full day to recuperate between stints. After her first week, all bets were off. She had it made!

Mama held that position for the next twenty-five years, helping develop a small Stale House business into the large retail operation it is today; redesigning the thirty-loaf boxes to fifteen, which cut the lifting by half, but increased the productivity.

My First Drink

A high school teacher and Minister was coaxed by Pastor Jesse into driving me to school. However, he wouldn't drive the one mile out of his way to pick me up at the house, so Mama had to drop me off on a street corner on her way to work, to wait for my ride. The return trip was even worse. I had either to wait for that same teacher or find someone else to bring me home. I wasn't getting home until six some nights. The grief of losing Daddy and the increasing homework was a lot to contend with. I couldn't relax, much less sleep at night. Six-thirty in the morning came quickly. One night about midnight, after I had finished my homework, I found Mama at the kitchen table sipping her wine after her hot bath. I told her I wasn't sleeping well. Without pause, she poured me an ounce of wine in a juice glass. I gulped it down.

"Not so fast! You have to sip it to get the full effect," Mama cautioned.

I immediately enjoyed a soothing, comfortable feeling throughout my body. Like a warm hug. Like a mother's caress.

"Better go up before it takes full effect," Mama suggested.

I put the glass to my mouth to taste the very last drop, then climbed the stairs a little woozy. That night was the first full and deep night's sleep I'd had in weeks. Thanks to Mama and her wine, it wouldn't be my last.

The nightly shot of wine didn't keep me from sliding into depression. By the middle of my sophomore year I was unable to see much of a future for myself. This was at the same time that my body was developing a will of its own. I shared with Mama some of the physical reactions I experienced, especially when I bathed, and her response was, "Don't do that anymore! That's a sin! You'll go to Hell!" She also recounted the many heaven-sent retributions I'd suffer should I persist to masturbate.

Mama similarly had disdain for news of the affection and caring I was receiving from some of the girls at school. I was excited about having girls talk to me and listen to my ideas. As we shared our dreams about our futures, I felt from some of them more than superficial curiosity, a deeper level of interest and sincerity. But Mama would say, "Honey, please don't let yourself get hurt. These girls won't be your friend for long. If you are ever going to find someone for a relationship, she will have to be handicapped like you. It can't work with those (normal) girls."

This was the worst news imaginable! "Why?" I pleaded, almost overwhelmed with sadness.

"Because that's the way life is! Normal people with normal people, handicapped with handicapped people."

Was it true? Is the world as cruel as she implied? Mama was always right. So, I concluded, "If my life is going to be this painful, I'll just have to make the best of it." But as determined as I was to not fall into self-pity, my decline was sure and steady.

By all appearances, I was OK. I managed to keep up with school work. I involved myself in activities, like the Audio/Visual Club, to which I was elected President my Senior year. In the Drama Club, while my dream was to direct, I used my technical skills in two performances to control light and sound effects, building the light board from scratch.

But, as graduation approached, and my classmates dreamed their dreams of college or a good secure job in business, my train had reached the end of the line. With no steam left in my engine, I felt college was out of the question. Still, in the recesses of my being, there was the memory of what Grandpa Hennicken had said to me, "There be a million dollars out there waiting for you."

I had never had to earn a cent in my first nineteen years. What I faced now was a world without ready-made opportunities for making a living, much less, building self-sufficiency. If I was to "make it," I'd have to invent the process.

The Process Of Inventing The Process

After wasting most of the summer sleeping in and watching television, I decided to explore Vocational Rehabilitation, a state agency that helped people with disabilities either go to school or start small businesses. Feeling some hope and anticipation, Mama and I made the trip into downtown Detroit in late August. Following a battery of tests, my interviewer, Mrs. King, sent us home to await a follow-up evaluation, which was scheduled for two weeks later. I had hoped to walk out that day with some support to start a business of my own, a hobby shop, perhaps.

At my follow-up appointment, Mrs. King looked at my file and said, "Philip, the tests results show you to be a very bright young man. Now, tell me what you would like to do with your life?"

"My life?"

I thought to myself. I thought I had already told her about running a business like a hobby shop. I looked at Mama, then back to Mrs. King.

"Philip, tell me something you would be interested in doing with your life?" Mrs. King asked again.

"I want to own a hobby shop and sell toy trains and model airplanes. I know there is big money in hobbies," I stated with authority. "The only difference between men and boys is the price of their toys," I threw in for good measure.

No reaction. Mama awkwardly smiled at Mrs. King. Mrs. King looked away from Mama, back to me, then down, as she thumbed my file. Her chin resting in the palm of her left, she sighed, and looked up at Mama and addressed her, though talking to me.

"Well ... I, I don't think you are able to run something like a hobby shop. There is so much paper work to be done. You would have to do all the ordering of supplies, all the book work and, most important of all, how would you wait of your customers? You might scare them away with your CP. By our criteria, you really aren't suited for that kind of work."

Though I couldn't say the words, I protested, feeling like I was fighting for my life. "What do you mean, I *can't!* How can you say I'm not suited, when I've been around construction, modelling, trains and crafts for nearly twenty years! I'd scare away the customers! I have to hide myself because I have CP and that frightens people! How dare you! How cruel! How narrow-minded of you! How absolutely wrong you are!"

None of this was said. I stuffed all of the anger. But I wanted to die! Mama accepted the judgment on her own terms.

Jogging the contents, then closing the folder cover, Mrs. King ended my review, "A hobby shop is definitely out of the question, Philip." To Mama she said, "I don't see much we can do for your son, Mrs. Schmucker. Our criteria tell us Philip could consider himself very lucky if he could sell newspapers in a newsstand."

The long ride home that afternoon brought back the same lost feelings I felt the night Mama and I drove home from the hospital. Once again, I was staring out the car window watching humanity pass me by. Drained by the interview, I gave in to the steady rhythm of the tires on the pavement strips, and I slept.

Perhaps Mrs. King was right. After all, I had started a lot of little businesses during the years, but I never stuck with any of them. They became a drudgery, I needed a lot of outside help, or I had so many other restrictions on me at the time, I just lost interest.

My first business was making and selling hot pads. With materials from an art store, I wove an array of unique patterns. After a good deal of frustration with my own handwriting, I arrived at my costs and came up with a pricing strategy of two hot pads for a quarter. I then took my stock door-to-door in my neighborhood, selling out and taking orders for more. However, I quickly saturated the neighborhood, because Mama didn't want me to venture too far from home. For that reason, and out of my own lack of self-esteem, I was out of the hot pad business.

When one of my classmates showed off a sixteen-point Christmas star made from strips of paper, that was dipped in hot wax and sprinkled with glitter, I was hooked! My classmate wouldn't share where to obtain the materials or any other details of the process. Working from a diagram in an art magazine, I had Mama cut multicolored wrapping paper (which made a prettier star than the plain solid colored strips my classmate used).

Then, I set up a real assembly line in the corner of the basement. It started with the folding area, from which the folded stars moved along an overhead conveyor of string to the hot wax dip, which proceeded to an area where I sprinkled the glitter on the wet wax, after which, the stars hung on a line to dry. They were a bargain at two for a quarter, and I soon sold out. But I soon lost interest, because the time and effort to make them didn't seem worth the price.

My biggest early enterprise was Christmas wreath sales. My Uncle Al was a florist. He suggested, "You could really make some big money selling Christmas wreaths, Philip." My first Christmas, with Daddy's help, I sold 500 wreaths, making one dollar apiece. The next season, Daddy pushed me to go door-to-door for orders beyond our immediate neighborhood. Each day, Daddy would come home from work and demand an accounting of how many new orders I had in my order book. When there was only two or three, all hell broke loose. Nothing less than the best was ever good enough for Daddy....

I felt a nudge on my shoulder. "Honey, we're home," Mama said. "Wake up."

"Home?" I woke as remnants of my dream continued to filter in and out of my mind, a million dollars dancing to a triumphant march to celebrate my future success.

IN A STATE OF LIMBO

One late August afternoon, I was sitting on the front porch drinking a Pepsi and trying to look "cool" smoking a cigarette. I watched a neighbor across the street come home from his day of landscaping. A Hungarian immigrant who had fled to America in the mid-1950s, he supported himself then going door-to-door cutting lawns with one lawn mower. Five years later, he had a pickup truck and a trailer loaded with power equipment, plus a crew of five working for him. The idea came to me like a bolt of lighting. I'll sell Christmas wreaths again this season, buy a power mower with the profits and cut lawns next summer!

The plan worked like a charm. That spring, I bought the best self-propelled reel-type mower I could afford, because I felt a reel-type mower did a better job of cutting the grass. I had three customers lined up before I realized I had no way to transport myself and my equipment.

Don Makemson, Daddy's former assistant at the bakery, came to my rescue. He fabricated a dolly I could hitch on the back of my oversized tricycle. It was hard pedaling the fully loaded dolly down the sidewalk, but I was satisfied with my profits of fifteen dollars a week, a decent chunk of change in the early '60s. But I wasn't cut out to do heavy landscaping. By fall, I was glad the summer season was over, although I had no good plan for the following summer.

Fall and winter came and went. Although the future looked pretty bleak, a part of me was still hanging on to my million dollar dream. On a rainy afternoon in mid-April, the phone rang. I was home alone. Mama was at work. Grandma was off shopping. Michael, Linda, and Laurie were in school, of course. To my surprise, the caller wanted to speak to me. He represented the Cerebral Palsy Association.

"The League For the Handicapped is starting a new program. It's geared for people like you, Philip."

"People like me?" I thought.

"They asked us to submit some names of people we think could benefit from the program, and you are on the list. We think it will be good for you to enroll in the program. It will test you and determine what kind of work you are suited for."

I was ecstatic! Finally someone is going to take a look at me and recognize my many talents! I waited almost a month before I received their letter. It was addressed to a Mr. Shoemaker. It said I was to begin my four-week evaluation on the following Monday. But how would I get there? A city bus? I didn't know the bus routes! In fact, I had never ridden a city bus in my life!

Mama helped me make a plan. Monday morning, I cycled to a neighbor's gas station located on the downtown bus line. Even with two transfers, the bus ride proved to be less of a challenge than I feared. I arrived at the League to find myself among a group of strangers, until I recognized someone I hadn't seen since grade school, my closest friend, Michael! He was as excited to see me, as I was to see him. We did a lot of catching up with one another after these last five years.

Referred to as "clients," our first week was test after test. Michael and I weren't exactly thrilled, but we went along, because getting a real job was paramount. Our second week was divided into a series of pretend workshop settings. These were far different from Daddy's workshop at the bakery.

My first pretend job was counting nuts and bolts, putting them into small packages. After lunch, I reversed what I had done, dumped out the package contents and resorted the nuts and bolts. In another workshop the next day, I disassembled a carburetor, reassembled it, disassembled it, and so on. Later, in an office setting, I operated an antiquated hand-crank adding machine. Why this old and difficult-to-operate office equipment was being used for testing in the dawning days of the electronic office, I was never told.

Finally, our four weeks were over. As Michael and I waited for our evaluations, we watched the excitement in the new faces of those who had come in to fulfill their dreams. As Michael and I compared notes, a job counselor called: "Mr. Shoemaker! How are you today?"

"That's S-C-H-M-U-C-K-E-R not S-H-O-E-M-A-K-E-R. Other than that, I am fine," I said as I walked to his desk.

He began to thumb through my file like Mrs. King, shuffling the papers with a blank, "just doin' my job" expression.

"Oh, yes. I see. Well, we have the results of your evaluation. But I'm sorry to say the results aren't very good. Due to your Cerebral Palsy, there doesn't seem to be much you are capable of doing."

"What *can* I do?" I asked anxiously.

"Well, you might be able to sell newspapers in a newsstand."

Michael said he was given the same evaluation.

When I got home, I broke my "rule" about drinking only one glass of wine and only before bed, and I went straight for the fridge and poured myself a tall glassful. Wow! Instantly, my anxiety vanished!

Later, Mama and I talked about my feelings about wanting to do something less strenuous than cutting lawns, but how I had hoped it would be something better than selling newspapers. Mama offered to call the first of the two local newspapers. *The Detroit News*, was very cooperative until she explained I had Cerebral Palsy. They flatly refused. The second paper, *The Detroit Free Press*, said they'd send an interviewer out the next morning.

Mama was at work when he arrived. But thank God Grandma listened in, because as the man expressed his doubts about me, she spoke right up.

"What's wrong with you people? Is no one ever going to give the kid a break? Are you telling him he can't do anything? You have no idea what this kid has been up against. Besides, he has a younger brother who could help if need be."

"Well, OK, we'll give you a shot. I'll give you a corner about two miles from here. It's a very busy corner. You'll start tomorrow night from 6 p.m. to 10 p.m."

The next evening was cold and damp, one of those late May cold fronts was coming through. I pedaled my bike to the corner in the drizzle. To my surprise, I recognized the Free Press driver, Cam, who I met when I'd accompany Robert, my neighborhood playmate, on his paper route. I stood with my papers for a long time in the middle of the sidewalk in the pouring rain. People in cars stopped at the light seemed to be staring at me. When people started walking up and my papers began to sell, my fears eased. At 10 p.m., Cam came by. We settled up and I cycled home in the dark mist.

New Mobility

I soon tired of my nightly four-mile round trip. One day, I pedaled to the bakery to talk to Mama. Her Stale House had been expanded into a processing building as well as a store. Don was there at the time and overheard me complaining about the long bike ride. He offered to motorize the tricycle, which should lend itself nicely to a lawn mower engine. I bought a new engine with my paper money, and within a few weeks I had a whole new sense of freedom.

Before I could drive it, I needed a driver's license. Billy Jones, who worked at the bakery, put my motorized bike in the back of my Daddy's old Ford pickup and took me to the local police station. I passed the written test with flying colors. When it came to the road test, Billy unloaded the bike from the pickup, and I rode it in the station parking lot for the officer. Billy knew the officer, and he pleaded to give me a break. And so, although the officer was very skeptical, he gave me the benefit of the doubt.

"But, Philip, you must promise me you'll drive it only on the side streets."

"OK! Only side streets!" I triumphantly shouted.

I didn't hear the officer whisper to Billy, "I hope you know what the hell you're doing putting this kid on the streets."

Billy just smiled and drove me home. I maintained my corner for the rest of that summer. Michael helped me out many nights, taking the corner over completely for two more years.

As the weeks and months passed by, Mama made sure to remind me that I complained too much.

She'd say, "I'll bet your friend, so-and-so, doesn't complain about his Cerebral Palsy the way you do."

Even though I had more mobility than ever, and I had the newspaper job, Mama tried her best to help me see that these insignificant treasures were the limits of my lot in life.

I was also growing more depressed about my lack of privacy. I liked to sleep in the nude. And mornings, Grandma would throw back my bed covers, fully exposing me.

"You've got nothing to hide. You forget I raised your six uncles and your mother. Now, rise and shine. You can't sleep your life away."

Pastor Jesse also tried to help rouse me out of my moods with his lessons and Bible quotations. But these old formulas didn't work their magic for me anymore. Somehow I had a KNOWING deep within that I couldn't explain or express in words. Not to anyone. Not even Pastor Jesse. All my life this knowledge had been present. It was that there had to be something more to life in the universe than the vengeful, Old Testament God, Who had punished us for Adam and Eve and Original Sin. It had to be more than an empty tomb, and prophesies of judgment at the end of the world!

What it was that I knew and felt deep within me…only time would tell.

5
dreading the future

One evening, while Mama and I shared a moment over coffee after supper, she saw the depression in my face. As I stared down into my coffee cup, she said, "Honey, perhaps, the CP Center could help you get out of your depression. I think you should call Mrs. Schilling and talk to her."

"*You* do it," I snapped back.

"No, I can't do it this time. This is your problem. You're a young man now. You have to make your own phone calls and take care of your own business."

"All right. Tomorrow," I mumbled and gulped the remaining coffee in my cup.

Mrs. Schilling sounded like she almost expected me to call. I met her at her office a few days later. Although I had always felt intimidated by her, or her power, I proceeded to recite my litany of problems, when she cut me short.

"So, Philip, when are you going to move out on your own?"

I froze with fear. Move out on my own? That thought had never crossed my mind. Leave Mama and the kids? Can anyone with CP live by himself? What was this woman going to do to me!

Mrs. Schilling met with me weekly for the next six months. I slowly began to see myself differently. I saw my future in an entirely different way.

I realized the day would come when I would have to move out of Mama's house. We were all changing. Michael, Linda and Laurie were growing up, too. Mama was dating. Besides, I was managing my own money better. I was even banking my Social Security check. I made money selling my papers. And I had started paying Mama room and board.

Mrs. Schilling encouraged me to take a few first steps by getting out of the house, going to a movie or an auto show. She also encouraged me to develop a social life through the Adult CP group. I was still going to the Handi-Teen-Capps. She pointed out I was no longer a teenager, and that some of us older ones at the teen club were stuck in our past.

I called my buddy, Michael.

"Hey, Mike, let's go the Adult CP Club Friday night."

He agreed. The Center provided transportation. At first, we were both put off when we discovered the meetings were held at the League For The Handicapped. We had never wanted to set foot in that place again. But, here we were, back in the cafeteria, which had been set up with two pool tables, two ping-pong tables, a piano, and other adult amenities.

During the evening, I noticed a cute ash blond sitting on a couch, talking to a man. I felt an instant and powerful attraction to her. I thought she was the most beautiful woman with CP I had ever seen, but I was too shy to walk over and introduce myself. I discovered her name was Joyce, and the man she was speaking with was her boyfriend, George. After that night, Michael and I returned monthly. When we heard about the annual Christmas Party they were planning, we made plans to go.

The night of the party, when I got into the car that would take me there, Joyce and George were in the back seat. Never had I seen her look so attractive. It was all I could do to contain myself as I sat next to her. When she took off her coat at the club, I couldn't believe my eyes. Joyce wore an elegant, low-cut floral gown. While most women with CP felt like hiding their beauty, Joyce did not. I remember staring at her the entire evening.

I had no intention of stealing Joyce away from George. Besides, Joyce lived on the east side of the city. She might as well have lived in China! It would take forever to drive my bike to her house. Still, it was difficult sitting across the table from a woman I so desperately wanted to know.

Adding to my frustration that night was the way all of my new friends were drinking alcohol as if it was water. I didn't want to drink in public, because I already began to understand what the wine was doing to me. Even then, when I arrived home, I took my nightly dose of wine, which was now up to two-and-one-half juice glasses. And to bury my growing desires for intimacy, I poured myself a third glass, and toasted Joyce, my secret love.

Ice Cream Man

I continued to counsel with Mrs. Schilling through the late winter. The paper corner wasn't cutting it. I hated standing out in the cold. It certainly took some time before I got used to being stared at. Even more, it was less than I was capable of doing. The idea of an ice cream truck was in the back of my mind. Later, I told Mrs. Schilling about my dream, I expected the response I had received from Voc Rehab, but she surprised me.

"You can't sit on this dream the rest of your life," she said firmly. "If you don't check the possibility of being an ice cream man, the thought will haunt you the rest of your life. Go back to Voc Rehab and see if they will help you get an ice wagon or something that will allow you to sell ice cream."

She knew the thought of going back to those people petrified me, but she insisted. I very reluctantly went to meet with Mrs. King. I explained my money scheme and she listened. But with all of that, her response was more of the same.

"Philip, I still can't see how you think you can sell ice cream. To drive a small scooter you need a driver's license."

"I got one!" I shot back.

"Oh?" she inhaled, caught off-guard.

"Yeah, I got one to drive my motor bike!" I said with pride.

Shocked, she demanded, "And where did you get a motor bike?"

"I had it built!" I said in a sarcastic tone.

"Well! Even at that, I still don't see any way we can help you. We can only help those clients we feel are a sure thing. Again, your records with us and those we received from the League show you to be highly unlikely to become a successful ice cream man. I am sorry!"

This time I didn't feel defeated. I left Mrs. King's office feeling triumphant, empowered to become an ice cream man! Thanks again to Don's ingenuity, the box was ready in no time. It was well-built and sturdy, painted white, with a door on the top. It hitched like a trailer to the back of my bike. Jimmy, one of the bakery office managers hand-lettered it: PHIL'S ICE CREAMS.

As the costs of this venture mounted, my resources dwindled to almost zero. What's more, it would cost another fifty dollars for the vendor license. I thought, perhaps, this was one thing Voc Rehab should do for me, so on my own, I called back.

"You are persistent, Philip," Mrs. King said. "Maybe you are different. We will pay for your vendor license, but we can't pay for the ice cream box because it is homemade."

"Fine," I thought. "At last there is something coming from Voc Rehab!"

Things were falling into place, as if there was a strange power making everything happen when it was supposed to happen. The final touch I required for my ice cream wagon was a unique bell. I located a genuine ship's bell, which I fastened to the front of the box with a pull string from the clapper to my handlebars. Presto! I had a very different sounding bell, so the kids would know that Phil, the ice cream man, was coming.

Buying the ice cream was my next hurdle. The depot was a six-mile drive from Mama's house. Again, Koepplinger's came to the rescue. A member of the Lutheran church, one of Daddy's old drinking buddies, Arnie, was in recovery from alcoholism. Just before he died, Daddy helped get Arnie a night job loading Koepplinger delivery trucks. When Arnie heard of my need, he offered to take me to the ice cream depot after he got off work, about 11 a.m., which was perfect timing!

The very last hurdle was getting dry ice. I could pick it up at the ice cream depot, of course, when Arnie took me there, but how would I get it when I didn't need to get the ice cream? The simple answer was the milkman. Our milkman delivered dry ice right to our milk chute! And I was only supposed to be qualified to sell newspapers from a street corner?

Within no time, my ice cream business was booming! When I wasn't driving through neighborhoods, I rotated between three schools, where I established myself at strategic corners, just as the schools let out at noon, and then after school. I raked in the change as fast as my hands would allow. In time, my corners became so lucrative, Good Humor tried to squeeze me out. I solved that marketing problem with permission from the schools to set up right outside the doors on the school grounds.

Business increased so quickly, I soon outgrew the capacity of my ice box. More seriously, my bike motor was proving to be underpowered for the job. Also my clutch bearing kept burning out. But it happened that Eddy, a neighbor across the street, who was a toolmaker at GM, could make bearings for me as fast as I wore them out.

After the season, I used my first year's profits to buy a Cushman Scooter, like Meter Maids use today, and Don built me a larger capacity ice box. Next season, I'd drive myself to the depot and load up just like the other ice cream vendors.

Is It Jackie?

With Joyce out of reach, I kept looking for that certain someone. It was during this time that one of my special school classmates, Jackie, and her family, moved into our neighborhood. I had always thought we could have something going between us, and now that might be possible since I could drive to her house on my scooter. When I called to ask Jackie out to a movie, she answered.

"Hello?"

"Hi, this is Phil. Would you like to go to a movie with me?"

"Well, I guess so," she said with doubt in her voice. "But, how will we get there?

"I can ride my ice cream scooter to your house. From there we can take a cab."

The following Friday evening, when Jackie answered the door, I wanted to hug her, but didn't know how to ask. I went in and called the cab. The cab ride proved to be more expensive than I had anticipated, but this was the way it had to be if I was going to date Jackie. Cab rides to and from the movies don't present much of an opportunity for romance.

The movie we saw become one of my all-time favorite films, *In The Heat Of The Night*. Standing under the marquee waiting for a cab to take us home, I remember telling Jackie, "This movie is sure to win the Academy Award for Best Picture." In fact, it won Best Picture, Best Actor, and other awards that year. Back at Jackie's house, she gave me a good night kiss on the cheek. I never did get my hug.

After that night, I began seeing Jackie on a regular basis. Over the summer, our relationship developed as we shared dreams that every man and woman dream. We even discussed how our CP would create obstacles to a long-term relationship, but we knew we could make it work.

Following the July and August doldrums for the ice cream business, when many families are away on vacation and the schools are closed, schools finally opened and my business began to pick up. One day after I had just returned home exhausted from my school stops, the phone rang, and I answered.

"Hello?"

It was Jackie. "Hi, Phil. I have to see you as soon as possible!" She sounded very agitated.

"What's 'a matter?" I asked, not knowing what to make of it.

"I can't tell you over the phone. Just come over!"

"I'll be right over," I said. Without even cleaning up or changing my clothes, I tossed my money changer on my bed, locked up my ice cream box, and drove right over to Jackie's. She met me at the side door. For the first time since we had been dating, she was home alone. I confess my first thought was, "Oh, boy!" But she sat right down at the kitchen table and started to talk. I did the same.

With a quivering voice she said, "My mother has decided to move back to upstate New York, where she and daddy are from."

I was in shock. "Any chance of her changing her mind?"

Shaking her head, she went on, "That's why I'm home alone. She's in New York right now, looking for a house."

There was nothing more to say, except, "Good bye." With tears in our eyes, we hugged one last time. Before the end of the following week, Jackie was out of my life forever. I fell into a deep depression. Jackie had been my incentive and now she was gone. I let my ice business go downhill. I began sleeping in, moping around the house like I had several summers before, and I increased my nightly intake of wine. Mama had paid little attention to my relationship with Jackie. But I hadn't shared much, remembering her reaction to the "puppy love" incident with Kathy in the fifth grade. What Mama did notice at first, she must have felt I'd get over. Or, perhaps, she thought I'd rebound in the spring, when my business normally picked up. Well, I didn't pick up that spring. That's when Mama became concerned.

Phil And The Magic Pill

Unknown to me, Mama took one of her precious Wednesdays off to see my counselor, Mrs. Schilling.

"Not to worry about Philip. He will make it in life. We all do, sooner or later," were Mrs. Schilling's comforting words for Mama. "There's nothing you can do to change the way Philip is thinking. Best thing for you to is get on with your life."

Mama did have her own needs. She was still young, and very attractive. She deserved a life with a committed companion.

On a warm June afternoon a few weeks after Mama's visit with Mrs. Schilling, the phone rang, and I answered it.

"This is Tom from the CP Center. Mrs. Schmucker, please."

"Hi, Tom. She's working," I droned.

"Is this you, Philip?" he asked, puzzled by my improved speech over the phone. "I was calling your mother to tell her about a new wonder drug that is supposed to cut down on the spastic movements associated with CP. I wanted her permission for you to try it. Have her call me when she gets home."

"I'll give you the number at the bakery. You can call her there," I offered.

"Fine. I'll do that."

The following Wednesday at the CP Center, Mama and I were taken into a makeshift examining room, where Mrs. Schilling, Dr. Raymond Bauer, an M.D. Neurologist, and two associates were seated at a long table. Dr. Bauer explained that they were doing research on a new drug. Their plan was for me to start taking one 10mg capsule once a day for five days, then to double the dosage for five days, and so on, until the "right" level was obtained. No prescription would be written, Mrs. Schilling simply handed Mama a bottle containing 100 capsules.

Within a couple hours of taking the first capsule that evening, I could feel its effects. The next day I thought I could use my hands a little better than the day before, especially when I had to make change while selling ice cream. Mama and Grandma both said they noticed a change in my behavior, too, that I seemed less tense, was walking better and talking more clearly. After one month, the point of diminishing returns appeared to be three capsules (30mg) a day of this new drug called Librium.

During my next appointment at the Center, I reported the effects. "I feel fine. I can do things better. When I make change selling ice cream, I am not so tense."

"Your speech is clearer, as well," Dr. Bauer smiled. "This month, let's see what the differences are, when you stop taking the drug. I want you to keep track of all of the things you notice."

The very next day, I awoke feeling tense and irritable. As the day wore on, the feelings got worse. I had to quit selling early, because I couldn't cope. I felt confused. By the time I got home, I was becoming alarmed. It was all I could do to call Mrs. Schilling at the Center. But by the time Dr. Bauer returned my call later that evening, I was climbing the walls! He said to take two capsules immediately, and to stay on the drug at 30mg a day until our next appointment. Within *minutes*, I felt better.

I met with the panel only one more time. They unanimously decided I should stay on the Librium at a level dosage of three capsules (30mg) a day, taking one or two more within a twenty-four hour period, if necessary. The CP Center would supply the drug in bulk form. Thanks to the panel and to these first three months on the drug, I remained hooked on Librium for the next seventeen years!

Librium does nothing, of course, to alleviate depression. And there were moments of deep depression when I talked of suicide. I had no idea if the Librium was accenting my feelings, or not. But, alarmed by my moods and my talk, Mama called Daddy's doctor, Dr. Ryan, who assured her there was nothing to worry about with Librium.

"Librium isn't the least bit toxic, Lorraine. It couldn't kill Philip, no matter how much he ingested."

For Mama, that was the end of that.

The Traveler

Soon there was a new man in Mama's life. John Migdel and Mama talked a lot about marriage. I didn't like John, because some of his behavior reminded me of the "ogre" side of Daddy, like his tough guy attitude with me, but especially his drinking.

John's latest and greatest idea was that our whole family would jump in the car and drive to California! What a great way it would be for him to get to know us — and us, him! I was the only one who thought it was a dumb idea. Six people, 3,000 miles cross-country during the heat of the summer in a car without air conditioning, and a four-week agenda of activity with only two weeks to pull it off! I almost stayed behind, except I was too afraid to stay by myself, and Mama would have been too worried about me to enjoy herself.

So, we all zoomed along on the "trip from hell." Our destination was Uncle Carl's, Mama's brother, in Los Angeles. After barely more than a pit stop at the Grand Canyon, we arrived late on the afternoon of the fourth day. Uncle Carl's pool was a refreshing relief for the Schmucker-Migdel family. The next morning, it was off to both Knott's Berry Farms and Disneyland. They left me at Uncle Carl's because I was a "problem." I think they knew they'd have to fly to see what they could see, and I would have slowed them down.

Home after our whirlwind family vacation, Mama and John agreed they could survive anything. The following October, Pastor Jesse married them, and we became one big unhappy family once again.

I did *finally* get my first chance to visit Disneyland four years later. With money I'd saved, I made my own trip out to Uncle Carl's and privately enjoyed his California-style hospitality, complete with frequent barbecues, a personal tour of LA and Hollywood, and a full day and night at Disneyland with my cousin, Kirk, at the helm of my courtesy wheelchair.

In the Magic Kingdom, I felt like I had entered another dimension of time. Walt Disney had died the previous December. I felt I knew the park layout pretty well from Walt's TV tours of his concepts and designs, and the park's construction progress. We began with Small World, where the entrance includes a clock called The Tower Of The Four Winds, which puts on a production every fifteen minutes, moving on from there. I recorded a lot of the music and sounds on my portable tape recorder to document my visit.

Dancing In The Streets

I never did like ice cream bells. From the beginning, I thought there should be a better way to attract the kids. My ship's bell was unique, but uninteresting. I tried a music box, but it played the same tune over and over. After I arrived home from California, I got the idea to add a four-track tape deck to my scooter so I could play the Disney music.

One late August Saturday afternoon, while Mama and John were away, and the kids were with Grandma at the lake, I disassembled a four-track tape cartridge to see how the continuous tape was wound on the reel. Then, I wound the tape on a empty reel and put it on my reel-to-reel recorder to dub my recording of the Small, Small World song. Then, I had to replace the tape back on the endless reel and reassemble the cartridge.

After 36 hours without food or sleep, I shoved the cartridge into the player. Excelsior! The music rang out at 7 a.m. in the clear Sunday morning air. I celebrated with Librium and three glasses of wine, then passed out for a well-deserved nap.

Late that afternoon, I woke, cleaned myself up, and went out to try my new ice cream music. I was less than two blocks away when I noticed that the kids were literally dancing to the music as I passed by! Surely, I was the only ice cream vendor in the city who could claim I could make the children dance! It was one of the most exciting events in my life. And because I had learned the secret of how to wind the tape on the cartridge, I could change the music at anytime in less than ten minutes!

Climbing The Walls

The combination of wine and my "wonder drug" took its toll on me. I found myself more and more tired and listless. There were times I wanted to climb the walls. I became disillusioned with everything and everyone around me. I needed a long nap everyday. When I complained to Mrs. Schilling about the physical side effects, she said I was simply being lazy, and she'd send me back home with another month's supply of Librium.

Everyone was tuned in to their own situation. Mama was busy making her marriage work. While I was deeply into my darkness, my brother Michael had escaped to Vietnam and back, and married his boss's daughter, which lasted all of nine months. Linda and Laurie also escaped the family. Laurie married George, the neighborhood bum, which lasted five years. Linda had the best luck of all of us, marrying a mama's boy! That marriage lasted 22 years before ending in divorce.

Santa's Toy Shop

Disney music filtering through the neighborhood triggered memories of other times, when I had made creative mechanical breakthroughs on my own that amazed those around me and made my world dance.

One Christmas after Daddy was gone, I finished a Santa cut-out for our lawn, which required pasting the image on plywood, cutting out the shape with a borrowed jigsaw, then mounting it in the yard on a pipe with guy wires. I later figured out a way to make one arm wave, complete with a motor, gears and counter weights. Using the same technology, including small Erector set motors, I animated my Nativity scene.

Motivated by what I had seen at Disneyland, memories of Christmas past triggered a new dream to build an animated Santa's Toy Shop. After September, I discontinued neighborhood ice cream routes and contented myself with my school stops. Later in the fall, I switched from ice cream to candied apples and popcorn, continuing those products through the winter. This minimal level of work activity brought in the few extra dollars I needed to work on my new dream. And since Disney hadn't responded to my letter offering my services, I'd show the world by recreating Disneyland on our front lawn.

Before I drew the plans for Santa's Toy Shop, I researched the motion and power requirements of the project. I knew my old Erector set motors weren't sufficient. I located suppliers of sophisticated small motors, timers, and relays to make this thing work. My inventory of music and sound equipment proved to be more than adequate. As I worked through the actual design process, my CP wouldn't allow me to draw beautiful looking plans, nor produce neat columns of dimensions and lumber requirements, but I knew what I was doing. My completed design was for a box with a four-by-eight foot face and rear, four-feet square on a side, with a gabled roof. The entire four-by-eight foot front was divided into two motorized doors on timers that would open up to expose the entire contents for viewing.

Mama didn't quite know what to make of my project. John didn't seem to much care one way or the other, except that I took over the entire garage. I worked every night, documenting my progress with Polaroids. One night, after I assembled the rough shapes and plugged in the motor, I knew I had a success. Sitting alone in the dim light, I watched the wide double doors of the toy shop slowly open and close on cue. I felt a presence with me that was sharing the triumph of personal engineering success. Visions of toy soldiers and elves dancing in the toy shop filled my mind.

The end result was a momentous success for me. The doors opened every ten minutes, revealing a merry-go-round of animated pull-toys, each doing something different as it went around. The lighting system was concealed in the gables, just like Disney would have done. The continuously running music was the March of the Toys, performed by The Boston Pops.

Among those who helped with the project, I include Virgil, a Koepplinger mechanic who fabricated the heavy-duty door hinges for me, and my buddy, Michael, who helped me keep going on the project, including the move from the garage to the front lawn. I also include Ron, the son of John's cousins, Harold and Marie, who worked with me while they and Mama and John played cards. Ron is visually impaired, so, there were moments when it was the lame leading the blind.

Santa's Toy Shop was a traffic-stopper. Ten seconds after the music began, the doors opened to reveal the merry-go-round of toys. In the back of the shop, Santa and an elf stood by a Christmas tree. The doors closed, the lights dimmed, then, ten minutes later, the cycle repeated. Some of the neighbors called TV-2 News. When the station didn't run the story at 6 p.m., I called the station. I was shocked, but not surprised by their response.

"I'm sorry, Mr. Schmucker, but my News Director, Joe Weaver, felt it just wasn't possible for you to build that display."

"What ... I mean, who do you think did it?"

"Well, maybe your father."

"Hell, he's been dead for eight years!" I snapped.

I lost it. All I could think was to call Pastor Jesse. I cried as I told him what happened. He said he had a friend at the station, and told me not to worry. He later called back to tell me the story would run at 11 p.m. with John Kelly and Jack LeGeoff. Sure enough. It was the feature story! The next evening, traffic in both directions lined our street. I was in my glory. People from all over the metro area braved the cold between the shows to listen to the music, watch the lights change colors, waiting for the doors to open. This was the best Christmas I'd ever experienced.

The following year, I had to top myself. I wanted to make Santa or the elves talk. I felt there had to be a way that the audiotape could be "cued" to produce this effect. Mr. Lark, the owner of a Hi-Fi shop in our neighborhood, listened as I described the effect I wanted.

"There's actually nothing that you can buy, but George at my other store might be able to come up with something." George knew exactly what I needed. He said he would build the switch, and only charge me twenty dollars for parts.

I recorded Mama's vacuum cleaner on one track to get the "tone" I needed to trigger George's switch, but it would not be heard. Then, from a script I wrote, I recorded Linda as the elf on the other track. After I edited the tape for precise timing: success!

Next, I enlarged the Toy Shop to install the switches and relays. Also, I found I had to heat the toy shop so all the mechanicals, including the tape player, switches, and relays would work in the cold. It didn't need heat 24 hours a day, only while it was running. So I installed a light bulb with a timer. The light bulb stayed on during the day to keep a thermostat at 70 degrees. At night, when the timer turned off the bulb, the thermostat cooled, triggering an electric heater that kept the Toy Shop warm.

At precisely 5:55 p.m., the timer kicked in. At 6 p.m. sharp, it was show time! The show opened with the chimes of Big Ben. The lights dimmed, and before the doors opened, an elf, lit off to the side, welcomed the children to Santa's Toy Shop. Then, the big doors opened, timed to the music. After revealing the merry-go-round of toys, the doors slowly closed as the elves sang, "Hi- Ho, Hi-Ho, Stay For Our Next Show." The show ran three minutes. After a seven-minute delay, it repeated.

The Toy Shop was large enough so I could climb in the rear, with all the electronics, and watch the cars going by, the expressions on the adults' faces, and the joy and happiness in the eyes of the children. That year, the Toy Shop was featured on the back page of *The Detroit News*, the front page of *The Detroit Free Press*, plus the 11 O'clock TV-2 News — all the same weekend!

A Panic Move And An End To Christmas

The Toy Shop sat next to the garage through the year. The following spring, as the neighborhood began to panic about the racial changes taking place in Detroit. Mama and John decided to put the house on the market. Just before it sold, they threw a cookout for their bar mates. John and his friends decided that the doors of the Toy Shop would make a good target for a dart gun they were playing with. When I saw them shooting at it from my bedroom window, I went screaming outside to stop them. All hell broke loose! John and I had a screaming match, which I lost!

The next morning, the Toy Shop doors were destroyed. I noticed an axe leaning against the garage. I picked it up and went into the garage to put it to the grinder, thinking I'd finished the job myself. In my anger, I ground the blade down to nothing. In a childish panic, I pitched the ruined axe into the neighbor's yard, but I never heard a word about the missing axe from John.

When it came time to move, John refused to take the Toy Shop. I painfully disassembled my creation, salvaging only the special audio switch George had made. I abandoned everything else, including all of the audio gear. I set my Nativity scene and my Christmas star aside, planning to take them to the new house.

The day of the move, there wasn't much I could do but watch. John, Michael and Harold, Ron's father, loaded the van, their efforts amply lubricated with a case of beer. I had been waiting to have my Nativity scene and my Christmas star loaded when Mama asked me to drive boxes over to the new house. When I pointed out my Nativity scene and the Christmas star were yet to be put on the truck, Michael assured me he'd take care of it.

At the new house later that afternoon, John and Michael arrived with the last load. I watched for my Nativity scene and my Christmas star, but they weren't there.

Anxious, I asked Michael, "Where is my stuff?"

"Ah, John and I decided to leave it on the curb."

In a panic, I drove the ten miles back to the old house. As I turned the corner, I could see the huge pile of junk they'd left on the curb. No Nativity Scene! No Christmas star! Someone had already picked them up. My greatest achievements, gone!

Five months later, on the Sunday after Thanksgiving, Mama asked me to put up the Christmas lights. Mama had the lights ready for me to put on the shrubs. I had no incentive for it. I had no interest in Christmas, for that matter.

"Philip, I don't know what's gotten into you! You used to love putting the lights up," Mama said.

"Ma! How can I enjoy putting your lights up, when I lost all my Christmas decorations?"

"Damn you!" she screamed. "When in hell are you going to grow up? That junk was for kids! You're nearly thirty years old. Grow up, kid! Now, get out there and put up the lights for me!"

Sheepishly, I went outside and did what she asked. Mama was right, as always. She knew in her heart, how much Christmas had meant to me. But she saw me as someone trapped in his past. She was at a loss to help me transform my life from a dream world into an adult world where reality was paramount, where dreams often didn't come true. At the same time, I saw the adult world around me and fought becoming a part of it. What I didn't realize was that my fight would culminate in a battle that would very nearly cost me my life and my soul.

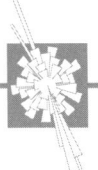

In an instant, the past, present and future blends into an infinite "Now." God spins around in his overstuffed leather chair and lays the transcript on His desk. He looks up at Patricia, who is waiting patiently by His desk for a reaction. Turning His eyes back to the transcript, He smiles,

"It's Heavenly! My thanks to the Transcription Department for such speedy delivery."

"I'll convey Your regards," Patricia says. "Other thoughts?"

God sighs, then rises to walk to his panorama window over the universe. "We are blessed in heaven to be in an infinite present. Linear time on earth, by contrast, past, present and future, is a creative playground for the will, where there are no rules. Individuals and nations, even religions, alike, who take it upon themselves to make the rules for others can make life a hell. Another potential curse is binding the self with delusions and beliefs, making up rules for the self that are impossible to fulfill."

Stepping back to place a hand on the transcript, He continues, "Philip chose to be born into such a narrow-minded culture with a body he cannot easily manipulate so as to not be able to fall lock-step into any corporate, political, social, family, religious, or traditional love pattern. Until this point in his life, as he tried to live by the rules of others, he failed in every respect to measure up, even within his family, with those that loved him most. That is about to change."

"Fascinating," Patricia says, taking more than a professional interest at this point. "Can you give me a clue, without giving away anything?" she asks.

"Simple, really, and very universal," God muses.

"Simple. Universal." Patricia repeats, not wanting to guess.

"A mentor," God responds.

Patricia smiles, "Every hero's journey includes the appearance of the mentor. But, isn't his father here with us?"

"Yes, of course. But the mentor is never the father."

Patricia nods, remembering, "As Karl Jung says, the boy must 'kill' the father."

God adds, "Jesus repeats the same ancient wisdom of the archetype when he speaks of marriage, when the child must cleave from the mother and the father."

"What a wonderful gift You are giving him!"

God looks up at Patricia. "It's not My doing!" He turns to the panorama view of His universe. "It's the archetype. I only set it in motion. It simply, always, will occur. Philip's mentor will appear, although Philip will not know who it is. And he may or may not benefit from his mentor's efforts, as much as his mentor may try."

"Free will. Philip is yet to learn that he makes his own rules," Patricia says to herself, thinking aloud.

"That is precisely what the mentor will first offer to Philip as a lesson. Remember, though, the mentor is not looking to find Philip. Philip will quite simply draw his mentor to himself, when he is ready."

God turns to Patricia with His hands cupped together. "When Philip is ready for what he thinks is his transformation, he will be most surprised to realize that his transformation is to see his entire world transformed!" With excitement, God opens His cupped hands and a giant Monarch butterfly takes wing!

6
new opportunities

One night in February Mama and John were out at their weekly bowling league, the kids and I were watching TV, and Grandma was in the kitchen doing her nightly crossword puzzle, when the phone rang. The conversation went on and on, something to do with me and a job. Who wanted to give me a job? And, if so, why wasn't I talking to the person? After about 45 minutes, Grandma hung up. The call was from Emmett Webb, a distant cousin of Daddy's and a long time friend. Emmett was always interested in what I was doing. Now, Emmett had an idea that would be an investment for him, while providing me a full-time job.

His idea was a unique, twenty-five cent, do-it-yourself car wash. Emmett planned to build it nearby, so I could maintain it. I thought it was a fantastic idea. I figured I could run the car wash and build up an ice cream route in the same neighborhood.

During construction, I really hit it off with Rodney Raub, who sold Emmett the equipment, and who was doing the start-up. I amazed Rodney by what I could understand and do. I learned what every piece of equipment was for, before it was installed. I learned how to diagnose problems and repair them. That was when Rodney himself offered me a job. By September, I was running *two* car washes. The jobs weren't time-consuming. In a few hours I could fill the soap tanks and towel racks, then take the rest of the day to sell ice cream. Sweeping the driveways at night was a different story. I hated that part, especially when the neighborhood kids would be out there throwing stones at me, the same kids who bought ice cream from me during the day.

Emmett thought I should work 365 days a year! No evenings off for my social clubs. No holidays. After all, Christmas, Thanksgiving, and Easter were the three biggest car wash weekends of the year. I thought people were nuts washing their cars on holidays. Eventually, Emmett relented with a night off once in a while, but I knew he wasn't happy about it. Rodney asked if I'd like to come down to his shop and rebuild water pumps. I jumped at that, too. So, now I was selling ice cream, running two car washes, and rebuilding water pumps for other car washes. In the off-season, when I wasn't selling ice cream, Rodney made signs for my scooter that read: Coin Car Wash Delivery Truck. When there were no pumps to rebuild, I delivered soap and supplies to different car washes all around the city.

Me, Drive A Car?

I was driving my third scooter, complete with a cab, heater, and automotive steering. After breakfast, I jumped into my scooter and hit the freeway. I did what needed doing, then hit the freeway, heading for the second car wash. By maintaining the minimum speed limit in the right lane, it cut several minutes off the three round trips I made each day.

Suddenly, there was a deafening sound under my seat, the sound of metal against metal. The engine had blown. I knew the little two-cylinder engine just wasn't built to travel fifty miles a hour. I managed to get the scooter up the nearest ramp, using the starter motor and first gear. I called Emmett, and then the scooter dealer, who picked up the scooter for repair

After the dealer called with the estimate of $600, Emmett said he'd make me a loan I could pay back with a $10 a week payroll deduction. Thinking about it all day, he called that night with a better idea.

"Philip, $600 is a hell of a lot of money to be putting into that scooter. For that kind of money you could buy a good used car."

"But, Emmett you know I can't drive a car."

"Who says?"

"Everyone. The CP Center. My doctor. Everyone I have ever discussed driving a car with says I can't drive."

"That's stupid! Hell, that scooter is almost the same as a car. I'll show you can drive a car. I'll come over tonight after I close the car wash. We'll go to the shopping center and you can drive my car around the parking lot. Then you'll see how easy it is to drive."

I hung up the phone in amazement. I thought of all of the possibilities I would have if I could drive. I remembered sitting on Daddy's lap steering the car down the road. Emmett showed me how easy it was. It was just like driving the scooter.

Back at the house, as I opened the car door, Emmett said, "I'll go out tomorrow and find a good car for that $600 you were going to spend on the scooter."

That night I dreamed dreams of success I had never dreamed before. Mama wasn't too enthusiastic, but she trusted Emmett's judgement. John was dead against the idea, but rather than discuss it, he just pouted in the basement with his beer. I came to feel that I deserved to have a car just like anyone else.

Late the next morning, Emmett came by, and off we went to buy me a car. Emmett had picked out a Ford Fairlane. The price was right, $600. But I felt lost behind the wheel, like I was driving a tank. As we drove around the block, I looked at Emmett in frustration.

"This car is too big. Why don't try one of those funny-looking Volkswagens?"

Off we went looking for a used VW. Behind the wheel of a three year-old model, it felt like I was back behind the wheel of my scooter, only better. Driving it was no problem. However, it cost $800. We took it. Look out world! Over the next few years, that car cost me more than $800, but the freedom of mobility it provided outweighed the costs.

DRIVE IT, OR LOSE IT

The VW gave me real independence. I could drive myself and my friends to the CP Club meetings. I had the car for dates. And I had reliable transportation for my busy work schedule. But I couldn't sell ice cream out of a car. So, the following spring I bit the bullet and had the scooter rebuilt. My ice cream business continued profitably for a few more years.

My VW also was a tool through which I learned an important driving lesson. For most of the year, I made my rounds shifting up from 1st, to 2nd, then 3rd on city streets, and into 4th on the freeway. When the first snow of winter came, all I could think about was having a nice warm vehicle to drive. At the first stop light, when I stepped on the brake, my car kept on going, only now it was going sideways. Then, BANG! The other driver got a ticket for drunk driving, and I got a $300 repair bill!

With the second snowfall coming down quite a bit heavier than the first, I debated about what to do about work. I had enough of that driving in snow stuff. After all, handicapped people really have no business driving in that mess. Of course, I knew better, but I expressed these fears to Emmett over the phone. As usual, Emmett surprised me with his response.

"All right Philip, I understand you don't want to chance wrecking the car again. That's OK. Take the day off if you think it's too dangerous for you to be driving today. On the way home from work tonight, I'll come by and take the car back."

"What?" I said in disbelief.

"If you don't learn to drive the car in all kinds of weather, you have no business driving ... period."

I was stunned. And the snow was piling up by the minute. I understood what Emmett was saying.

"Emmett, I'll be there."

"OK. Just keep the car in the highest gear possible. And on ice or snow, never use the brake. Downshift to the next gear or the next, using the transmission with the engine to slow down. Got that?"

"Yeah."

I grabbed one last cup of coffee, then left for work. As the car warmed up in the driveway, I practiced Emmett's driving tips before heading out on the road. After I made it through the corner where I had my accident, the tension eased. That day I drove through more than three inches of snow to work. I've never used the weather as an excuse for not driving since, which was some 550,000 miles ago — a lifetime of driving for many.

So Who Am I?

The person Emmett recognized in me is not the person most people see. I'm the same person. What Rodney or Emmett could see, and no one else, remained a mystery for many years. However, genius, talent, initiative, and hard work don't guarantee happiness or success. I felt inside like I was going nowhere. The Librium didn't quell the anxiety. And as the volume of my nightly glasses of wine increased, my inner voice was telling me I was getting hooked on alcohol.

One night, while John was in the basement drinking his beer, Mama and I sat in the kitchen having a conversation over our wine.

In the middle of another sentence, Mama said, "Philip, how many time do I have to tell you not to gulp your wine. Sip it like I do."

"Aw, Ma! This is the only way I know how to drink," I said with an exaggerated slur. I took another big swallow.

"Sip it, damn you!" Now she was off on it. "I don't know what I'm going to do with you! Thirty years old, and never have you been satisfied. Emmett bends over backward to give you a job. He buys you a car, and you hang on to that damn ice cream scooter, when you KNOW the car wash job is more secure."

I sat there staring into space as she rambled on. Finally, she got up, carried her empty glass to the sink, rinsed it out, and went to bed.

New Faces, New Experiences

After I finally convinced Emmett for some time off on Sundays, my friends and I explored other social outlets besides the CP Club. Myself and Joyce, Michael and Marian, began to visit the Metropolitan Activity Club. The MAC's Valentine Party was in an Elk's Hall across town. Somehow, I was elected the chauffeur. We arrived about 7:30, and before long the hall filled with over one hundred people, all with disabilities. There was singing, wheelchair square dancing, and regular dancing. I wanted to ask Joyce to dance, but I was too shy. I had the feeling she was making eyes at me all night, but I thought, "Why would she do that when she was in a relationship with George?" We enjoyed ourselves with conversation all night. After dropping everyone off, I got home around 4 a.m. and had a healthy wine nightcap.

I was impressed with the people at the MAC. The people who attended the MAC were different than my friends from the CP Club. These people were more sure of themselves. One in particular, Yale Adler, stood out from the rest. He was disabled with severe arthritis. His hands and feet were so twisted and contorted, it was a wonder how he could do anything with them. Our attraction was mutual.

Later that summer, Yale called after a Sunday MAC meeting.

"Phil, this is Yale Adler. You are just the man I've been looking for."

I was surprised by that. "I am?"

He asked, "You ever run a printing press?"

"In grade school we had a print shop. But, I was never allowed to run the press. The teacher thought I might get hurt."

"Well, what I am talking about is a bit different. Would you come over to my house tonight? I'd like to talk to you."

I had yet to make my nightly run to the car washes, but Yale's house was even closer to the first location than mine. I had no idea what he wanted to talk to me about, but I was excited. It would also be the first time I was in the home of a disabled couple. Yale's wife, Jackie, had CP, and they had three children. After introductions were made, Yale took me into his basement, which was dark, hot, damp, and full of all sorts of junk. Yale fidgeted with some old machine in the middle of all of this junk, and started it up.

"This is an offset printing press. This is the plate roller. This is the blanket roller. Down under here is the impression roller. Up here are the water rollers. And back here are the ink rollers."

Wow! I wasn't prepared to get a detailed lesson in offset printing, but I tried my best to keep up with Yale.

"Now, the principle of offset printing is that water and ink don't mix. As the plate turns, both water and ink are rolled onto it. Where the water sticks, ink won't, and visa versa. As the plate turns, ink is transferred to this rubber pad called the blanket. As the press feeds the paper through, ink is transferred to the paper from the blanket. The impression roller then pulls the paper through the press throwing it to the stacker at this end."

Yale could see that I was mesmerized with the whole process. "Phil, I have been looking for someone like you to run this printing press. I believe you can teach yourself how to run it and maintain it. The deal is, I'll buy all the paper, ink, and supplies you need. You can come here nights and see what you can do with it."

I was dumbfounded that here was a *third* person, along with Rodney and Emmett, who recognized my capabilities.

"I'll do it," I said.

"Fine. We can start tomorrow. Come over in the morning and we'll go downtown to buy the paper, ink, and supplies. You'll meet my friend, Johnny, a press operator, who can tell you more."

When I returned home, I shared my excitement with Mama, but her response was less than enthusiastic. "That's nice, Honey. But don't jeopardize your job with Emmett."

I came home excited about my future, but now I had the feeling that Mama was telling me the same message I got from Daddy and everyone else when I was little: that I must accept my disability and settle for what amounted to the world's table scraps. Sure, she loved me; but the little voice inside of myself that echoed her advice to stop complaining, don't get hurt, don't think, go slow, be satisfied, God will provide, was gaining strength. My Librium and my nightly glasses of wine could calm that little voice. But the stronger it became, the more I came to depend on my chemical helpers for peace and a sound sleep.

A STRANGE KIND OF DAY

Although I was anxious to get to Yale's the next morning, I had my responsibilities at the car washes. I also needed to pick up dry ice for my ice cream scooter. Still, I arrived at Yale's in plenty of time for Yale and I to make it downtown. Climbing into Yale's Suburban, I discovered that wherever Yale went, so did Jackie and the kids. I also found myself ankle deep in scrap paper. After some family bickering, we were under way, though there were several side trips, including dropping the kids at their respective schools. Finally, somewhere in the dark bowels of the city, Yale backed up to a paper warehouse loading dock.

From behind us, a voice yelled, "Hey, Yale!"

Yale seemed to ignore the voice as he wrestled with the steering wheel to maneuver the truck into place.

"Now, when they open the back doors, I want you to push all of this paper out," he barked at me.

I dumped the paper out as quickly as I could. Then, Yale drove to an adjacent building, where he maneuvered himself into another dock.

Another voice shouted "Hi, Yale!" and the back doors again opened suddenly.

I had to jump out of the way as two big boxes of printing paper were thrown into Yale's truck. The doors slammed shut. The man walked around to the driver's side. Yale handed him a check.

"This damn check better not be another one of those rubber checks of yours."

"Nah! I don't do things like that."

"You could've fooled me, Yale," he said as he folded Yale's check, put it in his breast pocked, and waved Yale on.

"On to the print shop!" yelled Yale, making his way back to the street.

There wasn't much I could do but go along with the program. I wondered just what I had gotten myself into. Following a side trip to McDonald's, plus several other errands for Jackie, we finally arrived at the print shop at about 4 p.m. All the while, I was wondering about the car washes and the soap levels. Emmett had been feeling let down by me, but, for the moment, I was trapped. As Yale pulled into an alley behind a store front, he laid out a blast on his horn. Within a minute or so, a man in his early forties came out the back door.

"Hey, how' ya doin', Yale!"

"Peachy, as usual. Johnny, I want you to meet Phil. This is the guy I was talking to you about yesterday. He has agreed to learn to run that old press I have in my basement. That way he can do some of the printing and it'll relieve you guys of some of my work."

"Sounds fine to me."

"Have you got my stuff?"

"Yeah. I'll put it in the back with the handbills we printed this morning."

Johnny opened the rear doors and shoved two boxes into the truck. Noticing the two boxes of new paper sitting there, he asked Yale, "What kind of deal did you cut on this paper?"

"Never mind. It's my deal, not yours." Yale handed Johnny what's called a paste-up and asked, "Would you take this job and show Philip how a plate is made for the press."

"You going to pay me in cash money? I really don't like all that rubber you've been giving me lately."

"What makes you think I'd do a thing like that? You know, Johnny, it's that IRS causing all these problems. Trust me, but please keep the check a week before you cash it. OK?"

"Yeah, OK, Yale. So, come on, Phil. I'll show you how a plate is made."

Late as it was, I followed Johnny inside the building while Yale and Jackie waited in the truck. What had appeared to be one store in the block of store fronts turned out to be one big room. There was nothing but printing equipment from one end of the block to the other! Johnny took me over to the largest camera I had ever seen. The lens stuck out through a wall, while the back of the camera was on the other side of the wall, in a photographic darkroom. Opposite the lens was a huge frame into which Johnny placed Yale's paste-up. Inside the darkroom, Johnny loaded a 10 inch by 15 inch sheet of photographic film into the camera back, exposed the paste-up, then processed the negative image in chemicals.

After the negative was dried, we went into another room containing tables with tops of backlit frosted glass. Johnny placed grid paper on the backlit table, then taped the negative to the grid paper. Johnny called this a "flat."

In another area nearby, Johnny placed the "flat" in a frame and placed a piece of thin aluminum over it, then closed the frame. The frame was placed under a bright light for about three minutes, which "burned" through the negative to produce a positive image on the aluminum. The exposed aluminum plate was treated with red chemicals which adhered to the lines that made the positive image. In the press, only the red lines would attract the ink.

"A finished printing plate," Johnny said as he slipped the plate, the flat, and the original paste-up in a envelope. "Now you know how a printing plate is made."

I had just witnessed the most exciting thing I'd seen since Disney's Tower Of The Four Winds!

When I returned to the truck, Yale and Jackie were waiting patiently. I had the sense that time wasn't much of an issue with these two. It was now about 5 p.m. I knew Emmett would be stopping on his way home from work and discovering there was no soap in the tanks. I began to worry. Yale said, "Phil, tomorrow I've got a man coming from Addressograph to check the press. He'll show you how it works. I want you to be there to watch him and learn more about printing."

"Yeah. OK," I mumbled, my mind miles away.

On the return trip, we had to pick up his kids. Once in his driveway, I jumped out and headed for my car in a panic.

"Sorry it took so long," Yale shouted from his open driver's window. "See you about 10 a.m. tomorrow!"

At the closest car wash, I found Emmett doing my job.

"I guess the only way I am going to motivate you to keep these tanks full is to knock ten dollars off your pay. You will have to do a better job to earn it back," Emmett said, as he tried to catch up on what needed to be done.

I really had nothing to say. The whole circumstance was feeling more like father/son, than employer/employee. Why didn't he just fire me and get it over with. I had lost interest, anyway. All I had on my mind now was that machine in Yale's basement.

I arrived home late for supper, as well.

"Where the hell have you been?" Mama demanded. "You have never been this late before? We've been waiting supper for you! Why do you worry me like this?"

"Ma! I am a big boy now, you don't have to worry about me any more," I responded.

"Yeah? Well, I'm still your mother and I can worry about you if I want." At the top of the basement steps she yelled, "John, we can eat now."

From the basement echoed, "Fine! Is your jerk son home now?"

"Yeeesss!" Mama hissed back down. "Come on!"

I was so stressed out, all I wanted to do was pop a Librium and eat. I really wanted some wine, too, but I still had to sweep the driveways at the car washes. I ate supper, then took a nap. At 10, I left the house to do my job. Tired as I was, the excitement and adventure of the day did not vanish. In my heart, I knew I was making the right decision. I was dreaming again of success and prosperity. A print shop owned and operated by two handicapped men! What a dream!

Running The Printing Press

The next morning, after servicing the car washes and buying ice at the depot to keep my unsold ice cream solid, I headed over to Yale's with time to spare.

I knocked on the door and Yale responded, "Come on in, Phil!"

Yale was scooting himself in his wheelchair toward the door as I let myself in. The family was still having breakfast. His two daughters were picked up by a neighbor and taken to school, leaving Yale, Jackie, and their two-year-old son, Allen, at the table. The house looked like a disaster had struck.

"Have something to eat," Yale offered, while trying to discipline Allen.

"Thanks. I already ate."

"The man from Addressograph called saying he would be a little late. So, that will give me and you a little time to talk. Let's go in the other room and I'll show you how I make the paste-ups."

Allen was hanging onto Yale's wheelchair.

"JACKIEEE! Please, come get this kid so Phil and I can go do some work!"

"He's your son, too!" came Jackie's voice from the kitchen.

I followed Yale into a bedroom he used as an office. The floor was littered with scraps of paper. There was "junk" everywhere, like the inside of Yale's truck. Next to his desk was a machine that reminded me of the toy typewriter Santa brought me years ago. Yale explained it was for setting type, and he showed me how it worked. The machine photographed letters one at a time after turning a dial. Then, the machine developed the words on paper. Cutting the words out and pasting them on another piece of paper created the paste-up. Graphics, like drawings and symbols to be used on the paste-up were also cut from old handbills, or other sources. Yale went on to explain all that went into the design of a handbill. I was so intrigued, time passed quickly, when our focus was broken by the phone. Mr. Davis from Addressograph was letting us know he was on his way.

"In the meantime, let's go down the basement and see if we can get the press running," Yale suggested.

While I cleared some of Yale's junk from around the press to give us room to work, Yale found an oil can, then turned on the power. At first it moaned and groaned, but with a liberal squirt of oil into every bearing we could find, it ran smoothly. By the time Mr. Davis arrived, Yale and I were feeding paper through. I was so engrossed, I didn't hear Mr. Davis come down the steps.

Mr. Davis looked at the press in amazement. "Man, I haven't seen a relic like this in years! Why, it's got to be at least forty years old!" As he made a closer inspection, "Seems to be all here. It obviously runs." He shut it off, then started it back up. "MMM...sounds great!"

"But, can you get it to *print*?" Yale asked.

"Don't see why not. Give me a little time and I'll have it printing in a jiffy."

"I'll leave you two alone, because I got some jobs to paste up for Little Caesars Pizza. I'm sure you can show Phil the basics of running this press," Yale said as he crawled up the steps.

"Well I'm not a teacher, but I'll give it my best," Mr. Davis said.

"Fantastic!" Yale shouted back and crawled up the steps.

Mr. Davis and I spent the next hour in the hot, damp basement. His hands had the grace of a surgeon. He disassembled it, readjusted all the rollers, put in a few new parts where needed, then reassembled it. Now, it was time to ink it and see what it would do. I learned to spread a bead of ink on the ink roller. Then, I learned how to mix the water solution. Then, I followed Mr. Davis' cues to affix the plate Johnny made the day before. I double-checked the paper in the stacker, and started up the vacuum pump. Mr. Davis showed me how to adjust it. A flick of a switch, and the press started to print with the quality it had the day it was built!

THREE JOBS!

For the remainder of the summer, I spent every evening, and sometimes afternoons, in Yale's basement, teaching myself how to run the press. I continued my job at the car washes, and hung on to the ice cream business, as well, although I seemed to spend more money keeping it frozen than selling the ice cream itself.

Emmett tried to motivate me by cutting my pay again, but that strategy failed. I was simply too immersed in learning the printing business to care about car wash soap. Each night, I showed Yale how I was improving the quality of my work. There were nights I would wonder what the hell I was doing, wanting to run and never see that damn machine again. Then there were the times Yale and I would daydream of our new venture, we called, "Handi-Printing." We even decided how we'd use reverse discrimination by hiring only disabled persons. We also discussed my need for more training in the print trade.

BUSINESS PARTNER, NOT CHAUFFEUR

By late summer, I had become quite skillful with the press. Yale was using my handbills, paying me per thousand. During this time, Little Caesars decided to expand dramatically in the Detroit metro area. It was very hectic for Yale. All his other accounts were put on the back burner to focus on Little Caesars, who came to Yale for all of their promotional printing.

By early September, I was giving most of my time and effort to Yale and only the minimum to the car washes. But even Emmett could see what we were doing. He backed off on pressuring me to stick with the car wash business and became increasingly supportive of Yale and me, and how we were going to set the world on fire with Handi-Printing.

However, the closer I got to Yale, the more included I was in Adler family business. I soon became the family chauffeur and errand boy, which had little, if anything, to do with building our business. When I mentioned this to Yale, he was quick to see what was happening. Jackie was upset because she had become accustomed to having me take her here and there, pick up the kids, or run errands for them. Eventually, all was forgiven.

Another important topic that came up was my need for formal training.

One evening, Yale said, "You know, Phil, we can't make this thing grow until we get you trained. I've checked around for printing courses in the area, and the only place that has an extensive print program is The League For The Handicapped."

My heart sank. "Nooo! Yale, not that hell again!"

"I know how you feel about the League, but, it's the only available program in the area."

"Well, then it'll have to be. I guess I can stand it for a while."

In A League Of My Own

This trip to the League was in my own car. Parking in the lot gave me a feeling of determination. I was also reinforced as I passed some of the same "clients" stuck in the same menial jobs around the building, including a "client" operating the elevator. Either the people running the League hadn't learned this job was gone, that all buildings had self-serve elevators today, or they were running a charity. Worse yet, remembering my evaluation more than seven years earlier, I passed new "clients" attempting to sort nuts and bolts, and operate the same hand crank adding machines! This was the dawn of computers and pocket calculators!

The suite of offices I headed into were in a new addition. After waiting a short time, a man introduced himself to me.

"Mr. Shoemaker, my name is Ken Monette. Would you please follow me."

In his office, I pointed out, "There is no shoe in S-C-H-M- U-C-K-E-R."

"Oh, yes. I see. Sch-MACK-er," he tried with awkwardness.

"Now, you said over the phone you want to take our printing course."

"Yes."

Mr. Monette shuffled his papers from one side of his desk to the other. "Have we ever evaluated you here before?"

"Yes, almost seven years ago," I said.

"Excuse me, please, and I'll see if I can find your file."

After Mr. Monette left the room, I fell into a fight or flight mode. He returned just as I took a deep breath to relax.

"Mmmm, your records show ..."

I cut him short. "I don't care what the records show. I am able to run a printing press and here is some of my work." At that point, I opened a file I had along with me and gave him samples of several handbills I had printed for Little Caesars Pizza.

Suddenly, his nervous paper shuffling stopped.

"I printed these after I taught myself how to run an Addressograph Multi-1250."

Again, he excused himself, taking my handbills with him. At this point I had *no* idea what to expect. My paranoia told me to expect the worst. In minutes, he reappeared at his office door.

"Mr. Schmucker, would you please come with me."

He led me down a hall of the new wing, when we entered a print shop. A young man approached us with one of my handbills in his hand.

He looked at me and asked, "You taught yourself how to run a Multi-1250, and printed *this* on it?"

"Uh, huh."

"That's what he claims," Mr. Monette threw in.

The young man gave a critical glance to Mr. Monette, then looked me in the eye and said, "I'd like to shake the hand of anyone with CP who taught himself how to run a 1250, otherwise known as the bastard of the industry, because of its complexity. If you produced this quality of work on a 1250, you are one hell of a printer!"

When he shook my hand, I felt really proud.

He turned to Mr. Monette and said, "Ken, I have never seen a person with Cerebral Palsy run a printing press. Let's give Phil a two-week trial period and see what he can do."

Monette protested, "But, Tom, our guidelines ..."

"Then, our guidelines are wrong! Give him a chance! His work speaks for itself. Look at his abilities, not his disabilities!"

We shook hands again, and I returned with Mr. Monette to his office. He was shaken by Tom's confrontation in front his lowly "client." He appeared to feel coerced to take me into their program, when I didn't appear to fit their damn profile. After a lot of rummaging and paper shuffling, I was officially enrolled.

"Your two-week trial period begins Monday. That will also serve as your new evaluation, since you haven't been formally evaluated in the last five years."

I was careful to say a polite good-bye. Then I returned to my car with my self-esteem at an all-time high!

The Excitement Begins

As I entered the print shop before class and introduced myself to the other class members, they couldn't believe that a man with Cerebral Palsy had been enrolled. Tom walked into the class just then and formally introduced me.

"Gentlemen, I want to introduce you to Mr. Schmucker. He's joining us for two weeks to show us what he can do. He taught himself how to run a Multi-1250. Now he wants to learn more. I think he's going to be a great inspiration to all of us. So, take those looks of disbelief off your faces and make him feel welcome."

Tom went about his usual Monday routine of handing out weekly assignments. At long last, he walked me over to a small press called an AB Dick-350. It was much smaller than Yale's Multi. As Tom showed me how to set it up for a run, I could see right off how much easier it would be than the Multi. I jumped on it like I had run it all my life.

Evenings, I continued going over to Yale's to run the Multi, turning out five to ten thousand handbills each night. Afterward, Yale and I would have another brainstorm session. I'd discuss what I'd learned that day and Yale would listen like the reassuring father I never had.

During my two-week trial, I had a taste of every piece of equipment in the print shop: the press, the folder, the darkroom, and the huge process camera. I stripped negatives into flats, and even burned plates. There was nothing in that printing course I couldn't do. Although I passed my trial period with flying colors, my setup times were slower than the other students.

On the last Friday of my trial period, Mr. Monette officially notified me I had been accepted into the 48 week course. I would have to wait until there was an opening, anywhere from two to six months; but that wasn't too disappointing, since I was already running the press every night for Yale.

As I left that day, I passed several new offices in the new wing, and noticed Mr. Wally Brown's office. He was now running the League. I smiled and kept walking, remembering the day he had told me I'd be lucky if I could find a job selling newspapers someday.

When I arrived at Yale's and told him the good news, he looked at me and smiled.

"You didn't have any doubts you would make it, did you?"

"I always have to keep proving to people what I can do! And I'm sick of it," I protested.

"Right now, Phil, what counts is you're in! You did it!"

"Yeah! I did it!"

DADDY'S TRUCK

GRAMPA HENNICKEN    THE HOUSE THAT DADDY BUILT

A YOUNG MAMA & DADDY    A YOUNG ME    GRAMDMA ZEHNDER & ME

HUGGING A FRIEND

DADDY & ME

ME, STANDING TALL

A PONY, BROTHER MICHAEL & ME

105

SHOWING SIGNS OF GENIUS
WITH MY STICK HOUSE

SCOUTING DAYS WITH DADDY

MY ICE CREAM TRUCK ADVENTURE

106

ME AT THE DOOR OF MY DREAM HOME

only two clients

Yale trimmed down the number of clients he serviced in order to specialize on the pizza handbill industry. Because his delivery methods were so unique, Yale produced a 20% response rate, when the national average was less than 1%. Little Caesars Pizza wanted an exclusive, but Yale held on to Domino's Pizza, as well. With only two customers, Yale was taking a big risk. During one of our nightly sessions, Yale got a call.

"Hey, Tom, glad you called. What? I'd like to help you out, but not until you pay for the two jobs I did for you last month. Send the money you owe me, and I'll jump right on this one. Sure. Call me again sometime, Tom."

Yale slammed down the phone and mumbled, "When we get established, we won't have to work for guys like him who pay late or not at all. Anyway, I want you to come along with me to understand the delivery side of the business."

Yale and I set out early the next morning to pick up "the paper" (the handbills) at Johnny's. Then, Yale headed downtown to pick up the crew at a rescue mission on skid row. The whole block was lined with vans from various organizations. Skid row residents would go from van to van for a job. It was an incredible scene.

When the men saw Yale's van, they rushed our way. I opened the rear door and the men shoved their way in. Yale had a good reputation with the men. Each man moved toward Yale to breathe in Yale face, so Yale could test for alcohol. If Yale smelled booze, his arm went up. "No! Not today!" Like a sad child, that man would step back and walk away. With eight to ten men in the back, we were off to deliver handbills.

"Hey, Frank, where do you and the boys want to stop today?" Yale yelled to the crew. Frank was a self-appointed team leader.

"McDonald's, Hardee's, or Burger King?" Yale asked.

"McDonald's!" they yelled in unison.

"McDonald's it is."

Yale pulled into the next McDonald's, gave each man three dollars, and they all piled out of the van. Yale gave me money to buy food for the both of us. I was embarrassed to follow the men into the restaurant, but I learned to get over it. In about thirty minutes, we were all fed and ready for our day's work.

When Yale stopped the van, the men knew what to do. Each man grabbed a handful of paper and filled his pocket with rubber bands. Yale gave final instructions from his window.

"Frank, you do these five streets here, then wait at the corner of so and so." Calling each man by his name, he told him exactly what streets to do, and where we'd pick him up. He also looked at the handful of paper they'd taken. "Boy, you sure scrimped on that paper, Ed. Better get more. And, remember, no mailboxes. It's against federal law!"

Here's where Yale was unique. He drove up and down the streets checking houses, and staying on the men to do their job. Other companies would just drop the men off. This is why he got such good returns for Mike Illitch. He made sure every house had a handbill on it.

One cold, snowy December day, while the men were out doing their streets, we noticed that one street had no paper on the houses. Yale pulled into local alleys behind the houses and businesses as if he knew what he was looking for. He found one of his men drinking a bottle of wine behind a dumpster. When the man saw Yale's van pull up, he cowered like a child.

"Hey, Bill, you got wine in that bag?" Yale asked out of the driver's window.

The man tried to hide the bag behind the dumpster.

"Dump it out, Bill, and get back in the van."

"NO!" came a sharp reply.

"Well, go ahead, then, and enjoy it, because when it's gone, you have one hell of a walk back into the city."

Yale rolled the window up and just looked straight ahead. "Watch," he said to me.

Bill stood there for a few seconds, and as Yale began to pull away slowly, Bill took one last swig, then ran after the van. Yale stopped and rolled down his window.

When, Bill came up to the window huffing and puffing, Yale asked, "Well?".

Immediately Bill took the bottle out of the bag and poured the wine into the snow.

"Fine," Yale said. "Get in the van, Bill."

"No, I want to work."

"Hell, you're too drunk to work. Get in the van and warm up." Bill opened the back door, climbed in, and huddled in the corner for the rest of the day. I was amazed how Yale controlled the men.

At the end of the day, Yale picked everyone up and dropped them at the nearest bus stop inside the city limits. As they filed out, in addition to their breakfast, he paid each man, including Bill, $3.50 an hour, plus bus fare to the shelter.

Lastly, he cautioned, "Stay sober tonight. And you'll work tomorrow." No wonder everyone wanted to work for Yale!

THE TRAINING BEGINS

My printing training began the day after New Year's. Mama and John had one of their holiday arguments the night before. But after a few extra glasses of wine with my Librium, I staggered off to bed and slept like a rock. My morning Librium, a little breakfast, and a couple cups of coffee helped ease my hangover, before I took off on my new adventure.

"Be sure to take your Librium to the League with you," Mama cautioned. "This is one time you have to be steady when you do things."

"Yeah, Ma. OK." I poured out a small handful and put them in my pants pocket.

On the way to the League, I serviced one of the car washes. I worked out a deal with Emmett that I'd do one in the morning, and Emmett would do the other.

In class on my first day, Tom put me to work on one of the four small presses. Just before morning break, Ken Monette, who was assigned to be my counselor, stopped by to see how I was doing. I knew I was surprising the hell out of this man. He was a "by-the-book" fellow, straight and narrow. He hardly said a word as he watched me work. As quickly as he had appeared, he was gone.

During lunch, one of my classmates, Ian, accompanied me to the cafeteria. He noticed the discomfort in my face and offered to carry my tray to our table. Ian was the son of a country doctor in northern Michigan. He knew immediately that I was taking Librium, when he saw the capsule.

"Phil, why are you taking that drug?"

"I have to. If I didn't, I couldn't run that press."

"But, that stuff is a depressant! It's supposed to relax you, make you sleepy. It slows down your reaction time."

"Well, that's what I want to do, to slow down my spastic movements!"

"I don't know about spastic movements, but I sure wouldn't want to be taking that stuff and run a printing press, or drive a car, for that matter."

"Well, all I know is I couldn't run that press in there if I didn't take Librium."

Our conversation stopped abruptly for the remainder of our lunch break. I remembered Mrs. Schilling and Dr. Bowers, the neurologist, told me I needed the drug. And I remembered the first day I went off of it, and those feelings of wanting to climb the walls. In my heart, I wanted to believe Ian. I didn't want to be dependent on a drug. Right now, I had no alternatives. I was hooked on the stuff.

At this same time, Tom noticed that I wasn't relating well with the other people in class, except Ian. Tom and I talked, and I admitted that I found it difficult to be open with other people. I told him that these were some of the reasons I had been seeing Pastor Jesse and Mrs. Schilling. He convinced me to get into group therapy twice a week to help me open up and learn how to relate to others.

A New Car

The VW I bought with Emmett's help was beginning to eat a lot of the money I was making printing for Yale and running the car washes. My choice was a new VW complete with air conditioning and AM/FM Stereo. On a day the League was closed for staff meetings, I cut a great deal on a new Beetle for $2,400 with $1,400 down. However, even with my good credit, the bank wanted a co-signer on the note for the $1,000 balance. I didn't want to involve Emmett, so I asked Mama. She was really proud of what I had accomplished, and she wanted to help, but she didn't know how John would react.

Mama figured she'd wait until later in the evening when John was settled down in the basement watching television and drinking his shots and beer. Able to hear every word through the heat ducts, I sat up in my bedroom with my fingers crossed. I feared the worst.

I imagined Mama sitting on a bar stool. In her little girl voice she said, "Honey, Philip wants to buy a new car."

"What's wrong with the one he has?" John asked, sounding distracted from his TV program.

"Well, you know he's been pouring all that money into it. It's time he had a new one. He has more than half for a down payment, but the bank wants a co-signer for the loan balance. I told him I'd go to the dealership tomorrow and co-sign."

"The hell you will, Lorraine!" he roared. "What the hell is the matter with you and your damn son! Don't the both of you realize he's nothing but a damn cripple, who Emmett is using to take that car wash job away from someone who really needs that job. The sooner he stops pretending he's somebody he's not, the better off he'll be. People with families to raise need Emmett's money more than he does. Damn it all! Lorraine, if you sign for that car tomorrow, I'm out of here!" The sound of breaking glass punctuated his threat.

For several minutes, there were no sounds but the TV in the background. Then, Mama let loose. "All right, go, you bastard! He's my son. Blood is thicker than water. I'm going to go with him tomorrow, John. I'm going to co-sign the note!"

All quieted down, again. I heard John's bottle opener pop open a cap, then the cap hitting others in a tin can. Nothing more was said.

The next day, when John saw my new car on the street, he picked up the argument all over again. He said he had meant what he said. The marriage was finished. At that point, I left the house and drove to the car washes in my new car for my nightly rounds. Afterward, I didn't know where to go. In tears, I just drove down the freeway, deciding after a long time to head over to Aunt Dorothy's and Uncle Les's for the comfort I so desperately needed.

When I arrived back at the house around 1 a.m., John's car was gone. The house was quiet. I had several glasses of wine and quietly went up to bed. The next morning, life went on as if nothing had happened. We all went our separate ways without a word about John. Later that day, when I arrived home, John had not returned. I felt terribly guilty that I had destroyed Mama's marriage.

Two weeks later, I arrived home from work to see John's car parked out front. It was all over. John had decided to return to Mama, along with some furniture he'd bought for his apartment, which ended up in the basement.

EMMETT SELLS THE CAR WASHES

It had been five years since Emmett built his first car wash. With the value of the car washes doubled, his objectives had been met. It was time to sell and reap the harvest. When Emmett broke the news to me, I was confused. I knew that he was mainly cashing in on his investment. But I also knew that my lack of interest and poor performance had affected the timing. At the same time I was greatly relieved to be rid of the long days and all of the running around.

All-in-all, I still experienced it as a loss. Even Tom at the League noticed my depressed mood. After some discussion, I agreed to increase my therapy sessions to three times a week. Also, the loss of income was still affecting me. In my depression, I medicated myself with increased doses of Librium and evening wine. My therapist overlooked the Librium and the wine, until I brought them up. He dismissed both, especially the wine, since I only drank before bed.

I LOSE YALE

Suddenly, my life felt like a freight train that had jumped the tracks, the cars piled one upon the other. The one dream I held on to was the Handi-Printing concept I shared with Yale. But, suddenly, even that dream was shattered. I hadn't thought about it at the time, but for several months Yale had been going slower at his work. He was even too tired many nights to talk about our business plans. I never let myself imagine the worst. But on a break one day, when I called over to Yale's to ask a question, his sister Kate picked up the phone. Nothing unusual, Kate was there many afternoons.

"Hi Kate. This is Phil. Is Yale there?"

"No, Phil. He was rushed to the hospital this morning with chest pains."

The news hit me like a ton of bricks.

"What's the word?" I asked.

"He's resting, now. They want to do a bypass on him as soon as they build his strength up."

"All right. I'll keep in touch."

The next morning at the League, I had very little energy. Then, just before the mid-morning break, I got a call from Jackie, Yale's wife, which I took in Tom's office.

"Jackie?"

"Oh, Phil. I have terrible news. Yale had a heart attack and died last night."

"What? How can a man have a heart attack and die in a hospital?"

Yale was buried before sundown that same day, so I never had the chance to say good-bye, much less mourn his loss at the funeral. I left the League before lunch and went home to our empty house, my Librium and my wine. I took several capsules and barely made it up to my room, before passing out on my bed for the rest of the day.

After that, my drinking increased from two or three glasses of wine before bedtime to four or five. Soon, I was drinking during the day to cope. I had relied all my life for motivation from my elders, from Grandpa Hennicken, Daddy, and Mama, to Pastor Jesse, Mrs. Schiller, Emmett, then Yale. I felt no self-reliance, no inner sense of direction. I couldn't think on my own. I felt very alone.

Rescue

My relationship with Yale was well-known at the MAC by the other members. Of course, no one asked how well our dream was progressing, but they all had their opinions. I knew some who thought it was a dumb idea. They didn't want us to succeed, because they themselves were not ready to look beyond the limits they placed on themselves because of their disabilities. Yale was known for his wild ideas, but the printing company run by handicapped people was the wildest.

One MAC member, who did not think the idea was wild or crazy, was Jane Webber, who was on the staff of Good Will Industries, a cousin agency to the League For The Handicapped. She believed in Yale's dreams. She had known Yale for many years and was encouraged by his creativity. She thought a business run by handicapped people was his greatest idea, yet.

At the time Yale died, she was just about to move to a new agency called, New Horizons, where she would head job counseling. She was anxiously looking forward to placing people with us in Handi-Printing. She was shocked by Yale's death, and realized exactly where that left me. Even with my League training, she knew the League would never place me, not with my CP. Without Yale, I had nothing.

Jane's concept was to have the State of Michigan's Rehabilitation Services set up a print shop within New Horizons. I'd have my print shop, and the New Horizons contract procurement people would obtain printing contracts, along with jobs for New Horizons. To spice up the package, New Horizons would launch their own printing course, and I would be an instructor. I went for the deal in a flash. Everyone thought it was a great opportunity. At the League, Tom even gave me lessons on setting up printing classes. But I was in no shape to be depended upon, much less to direct others in business or in a classroom setting. I was setting myself up for a major crash.

The print shop should have been ready in early fall, but it wasn't finished until the following spring. Finally, the big day arrived. I had my own print shop set up just the way I ordered it. However, the jobs that were supposed to come through New Horizons never came. One morning the contract procurement man walked into the print shop with a full-color flyer and asked for a sample. My heart sank, because I knew what was happening.

I said, "There is no way I can make a sample of a printing job. The only way a sample can be had is to set up and run the job. That's taking the paste up, photographing it, making the plate, running the job on the press, then taking a proof copy of the job as a sample. And full-color like this is beyond our capabilities."

"Oh," he said, not fully comprehending the problem. "Well, then how do I show the customer what we can do?"

I tried to explain, "All we can do is write a bid on the job and let the customer decide from our quote if he wants us to do the job. We show him the artwork before the press run. He can make changes if he wants. He OK's it. Then, we run the job."

The puzzled look on the man's face told me that the contract procurement people knew nothing about selling printing.

I decided to make our own flyer to advertise our business with area businessmen's associations. But where were we? On a dead end street in one of the worst areas of the city. We were not even in the phone book under PRINTING. Even the one little job I did print for a realtor was so poor because of my sinking attitude that the agent called back to say that he'd probably find better printing in a two-bit whore house!

After that experience, and with no other work coming in, I felt trapped in the shop. I'd sit at my desk, look around at all of this beautiful equipment sitting idle, and I'd cry. In mid-October, I had to let it go. I couldn't take the idleness and the frustration. I had someone take my IBM typewriter to my car and I drove home. I knew that I'd never see this place again. The dream was dead.

BOTTOMING OUT...ALMOST

One morning, less than ten days later, I couldn't get out of bed. My depression weighed on me and I couldn't move. I called to Mama in a panic.

When she came into my room I said, "Ma, help me. I can't get out of bed!"

"What the hell you want me to do?" she snapped.

Mama left me and called the therapist I was seeing. The therapist put the in-house psychiatrist on the line, who told Mama that it was imperative she get me to Northville Psychiatric Hospital, immediately. That jolted her into action.

Angry that I was interrupting her preparations for friends who were coming to visit for the weekend, she stomped back into my room and shouted, "All right! Get your ass out of bed, and I'll take you to the hospital. Now, hurry up!"

As she turned to leave my room, I could hear her complaining that she still had to clean the house before Chuck and Marian arrived. The additional guilt made it even worse. I could barely move. I was nearly paralyzed with fear. My arms and legs were like lead weights. I could'nt walk.

Using anger to hide her own fear, Mama helped me into the car.

When she turned the opposite way we usually took to go to the area medical hospital, I said, "Ma, you're going the wrong way!"

"Oh no, I'm not!" she barked back. "What in hell hospital do you think I'm taking you to?"

"Oh God, No!" I moaned.

Outside of the car, the world was moving backward. I saw my ideal self standing on a corner watching as we sped by. A store front opened up like Santa's Toy Shop, then suddenly slammed shut. I stood at a press as it spat out blank sheet after blank sheet after blank sheet. Jackie, who had moved to New York, pulled up alongside Mama's car in my new VW, looked at me, then passed Mama's car. Two children in the back seat waved at me. All was lost! From that point on, I recognized nothing and no one. I lost track of time and space. I wept.

Back On Earth, Still On The Bottom

I spent the next three days and nights under psychiatric observation. As I tripped out the first night, a tree outside my window tried to attack me. The next morning, while I watched TV soaps in a drug-induced daze, Mama was already working to convince the psychiatrist to release me into her custody. She, together with the psychiatrist, Voc Rehab, and New Horizons were planning my recovery program. Mama let me know how I was putting everyone out and how childish I was behaving. She demanded that I straighten up and fly right! NOW!

Jane Webber at New Horizons put the print shop on the back burner and hired me as a work shop supervisor at $80.00 a week. At last! A steady job with a weekly paycheck. I had only two weeks to come off of the drugs I received in the hospital. Using Librium and wine to re-regulate my feelings, I got myself in decent enough shape to start.

Walking through the workshop doors, I could feel the pain and the depression of the "clients," condemned to their sheltered existence. Jane sat behind her desk in her wheelchair and visited with me in her drab office.

"Philip, we're going to start you as a supervisor at minimum wage. You'll also be our in-house printer." After a little more detail on my assignments, the conversation turned into a lecture about how it was time for Philip to grow up and be independent. I listened to all of this, knowing her dependency upon her husband, John, and how truly trapped she was in her world.

I rotated jobs for several weeks. I watched "clients" do piecework, placing three washers and a nut on a bolt for a local automotive company. Another assignment was to build patterns called "jigs" for an agency customer, Bob Beader, a local hobby dealer. These wood jigs would enable "clients" to cut wood stock to size and easily position the drill holes so the pieces could be bolted together to form portable model railroad layouts. For a brief time, it was like I was back building Santa's Toy Shop again. In time, I was back supervising the three washers and a nut on a bolt group.

After six months of 40 hour weeks at $2 an hour gross, I was losing interest. Not only was the job jeopardizing my Social Security, which was more money, but it didn't seem to justify my effort or my time. The in-house printing never materialized. In the meantime, because the "clients" didn't care that they were performing repetitious physical manipulations, most of them made two, three, or four times more money. One payday, I lost my cool, and Jane Webber fired me on the spot.

I drove home defeated and dejected. Home alone that afternoon, I choked down a fistful of Librium with a fifth of wine. Mama found me that evening passed out on my bed.

"Why in hell are you doing this to me!" she yelled.

I saw how my depression was rippling through the family. Not only was John staying at the local bar after work, coming home later and later; but also Mama was struggling to do her job in the new Production Building where the original Stale House had been. In the front of the building, Mama, along with my sister Linda, ran the store. In the back, returned bread was made into croutons and bread crumbs. Ray Koepplinger, Karl's nephew, ran the company now. He and Lorraine were friends as well as employer and employee.

One morning, the gremlins were coming out of the machinery, and the stuffing department was fighting with the return store over the return bread coming in that afternoon. The store was low on stock and the production department needed to make bread crumbs. Mama was trying to manage the problems, when Ray called her on the intercom with his suggestions.

Her reply to his suggestions was, "Go to hell!"

Everyone was shocked, including Ray himself. Kindhearted, like his Uncle Karl, he cared about his employees. He suspected there was something under the surface causing Mama to act the way she did. In his office, they talked for a long time about old Mr. K., Daddy, me and the kids, but especially me.

After they had worked things through, as Mama was leaving, Ray said, "Lorraine, have Phil call me."

Mama was beside herself with excitement. She called me at home. "Honey, Ray Koepplinger wants you to call him this afternoon!"

I asked, "What for?"

"I don't know for sure. Just call him. Promise?"

"Yeah. OK."

I called Ray, and he asked to see me first thing tomorrow.

In my mind, with all of my memories of old Mr. K., Daddy, the other men, and everything good the bakery represented for my family, I felt like I was visiting a shrine. I went in the front door and climbed the new staircase to Mr. R. K.'s office, with its huge picture window that looked out over the entire facility.

Mr. R. K. greeted me, but we talked of the past for several minutes before he got to what he wanted to say. Maybe he was sizing me up. I doubt that he was as anxious about our meeting as I was.

"I had a long talk with your mother yesterday about some of the great things you have been doing, and some of the difficulties you're having finding something to do to make a living."

"Yes?" I replied, timidly.

"Well, I talked to the union and they are willing to bend a little so I can create a part-time job for you."

"I can work for Koepplinger's!?" I thought to myself. "All the years I wanted to work here, and follow in Daddy's footsteps. This was my Mecca!" I screamed inside.

I'm sure my excitement was spilling out, because Mr. R. K. began to smile widely and offered me his hand in a handshake.

"Tomorrow you go to the company doctor for a physical. Then, come Monday, you can start."

Working At Koepplinger's

On Monday, I reported to Don Makemson, Daddy's successor in the maintenance department. I was hoping all the knowledge in my head was finally going to be put to good use. As I walked in the side door of the garage, it was dark, even a bit gloomy, now, because what was once a wall of windows was now a brick wall of the new plant.

Don was sitting behind his desk when I opened his office door and said, "Good morning!"

Don said nothing for several minutes. He didn't budge from his paperwork. Not quite the welcome I had been expecting. I sat in a chair tucked behind the door and waited for Don's next move. Watching Don, I thought, "Is this the same Don who bragged about learning everything he knew from my father? Who told Mama that my father had been the best college he'd ever attended? Who motorized my bike and built my ice cream wagon?"

When Don did look up at me, it was a cold, hard look. He said, "Come."

I followed him into the supply closet, where he handed me a new push broom.

"Sweep the garage and loading dock," he directed, then headed into the bakery.

Alone in the bowels of the garage, I began to sweep. The job soon appeared to be overwhelming. The place hadn't been cleaned in years! Over the next few days, Don left me alone to continue the cleaning. As I cleaned, I'd wander around the garage area, just to see what was going on. Virgil was still there sanding and painting trucks. In the repair area, I'd visit with Bob, the head mechanic. Sometimes I would get a tool for Bob or, better yet, help him diagnose the problem, until Don spotted me.

"Bob's a big boy, Phil. You don't have to hold his hand. There's plenty of dirt in the loading area you can sweep."

Once, while I was cleaning up papers along the fence behind the buildings, out near the softball field, I had my shirt off to enjoy the warm sun. Don must have seen me out there on all fours and wondered what I was doing.

"What'cha doing, Phil?" he asked from the window of his pickup truck.

"Picking up all this paper," I said proudly.

"That's fine. But you missed quite a few little pieces back there behind you," he said dryly as he pulled away.

I had the very same feelings with Don that I had when I had wanted positive strokes from Daddy, and all I got was criticism.

As the warm weather took hold that spring, I began to hope that Don would let me do more of the spring and summer landscaping. The bakery had all kinds of heavy-duty power tools like edgers and trimmers and power riding mowers to take the backbreaking effort out of it. I did spend more and more time working outside, but not because Don assigned me to outside work. I was simply never told *not* to work outside. I should have sensed something, when I asked for a whip trimmer and was handed a brand new hand trimmer to trim the grass under the fence that ringed the entire property.

April came into full bloom, the grass became a lush green again. It was time to ready the riding mower. As Bob worked to clean it up and prep it for the cutting season, I helped to clean off the caked-on grass from the bottom of the shroud. Then, I drove it to the wash rack and washed it down with the power hose. I knew Don had seen me help get it ready, so I asked Don later in the day to give me a chance at running the mower.

He didn't say, "No." He said, "We'll see."

The next morning, I was sure Don would send me out on the mower. Instead, I heard, "Well, you better get busy and clean that dirt on the loading dock you've left because of all the time you've wasted doing other things." Not a word about the mower. A few minutes after that, another crewman, Albert Jackson, came into the garage, climbed on the mower, and off he went.

In the back of my mind, I felt Don's behavior about the mower, like the other power tools, had to be the result of some union or insurance issue. Then again, Don never said I could or couldn't, he'd said, "Maybe." Listening to the distant rumble of the mower echoing between the bakery buildings, I contented myself with the hope that Don would relent in time. I picked up my broom, chose a spot on the loading dock to clean, and tried to make myself useful.

CHOSEN

Everywhere I worked around the bakery, everywhere I looked, I saw traces of Daddy's work. He had built many of the old buildings, laid the brick foundation for all of the fencing around the property, built the baseball field, and more. Much, if not all, of the original machinery Daddy used had been abandoned in Daddy's old machine shop, left to rust and decay. As I roamed around his old tool storage area, I came upon Daddy's punch press. I reminisced about watching him years ago, how he could make anything Karl wanted, fabricating it from scratch, like the sesame seed sprinkling machine, that was still in use today, many years later.

Suddenly, I felt something strange, even eerie, like I wasn't alone. I knew there were no other employees within shouting distance. I became quite frightened and scampered quickly to the door. I stopped outside and turned. The presence was still there.

"I chose you!" Daddy's voice said without warning.

My entire body quivered. I didn't know what was happening. I noticed the rusted air compressor, silent, loaded with cobwebs. I looked around at the other machinery, hoping to catch a shadow. Perhaps, I was hallucinating. Perhaps, not. I returned to my chores knowing I wouldn't be able to share this experience with anyone, certainly not Don, and not even Mama.

8
you're never satisfied

Even with my halftime job at Koepplinger's to keep me focused, the days seemed to run together. I went to work for four hours, kept myself busy, came home for my glass of wine, and napped. After supper, I worked on my trains in the basement. Then, after the TV late news, Mama and I would have our wine together before bed. We never talked about much, but I wanted to. I wanted to share all of my frustrations. I wanted her to listen. But at the least mention of my feelings or problems, she'd criticize.

"By the way, Don tells me you aren't doing your work the way you should."

"Ma, I hate it."

"There you go again, never satisfied! You finally got a job at the bakery, the one you wanted all your life, and you still bitch. There is no place in hell where you could make that money for the amount of work you do. Then, you stupid son-of-a-bitch, you went and stopped your Social Security, like a damn fool!"

"I don't want to live off other people."

"Well, what's wrong with that? You are never satisfied! You always want to do the things you can't, and you do things you have no business doing! Your friend Dicky would give his right arm to be doing the things that have been handed to you!"

At the point that Mama would drag one of my friends with Cerebral Palsy into it, I'd pour another glass of wine, take my Librium and head to bed. Anyway, I wanted to be out when John came home around midnight and the two of them would pick up where Mama and I left off. If a year working part-time at Koepplinger's was a zenith, bottom couldn't be far.

I continued attending the MAC as a social outlet. It was not the same without Yale. At a September gathering, after I found a seat, I noticed a brunette with her hair cut in bangs. After a few minutes of glancing back and forth across the room, I moved to the seat next to her. Janis had only a very slight amount of Cerebral Palsy. As we talked that afternoon, ignoring everything else that was going on, I felt something in her eyes I hadn't felt since Jimie moved away. I drove her home and arranged a movie date for the following Tuesday.

When I saw her waiting at her door in a miniskirt, I knew tonight would be a first for me. I missed most of the first half of *Fiddler On The Roof*, because I kept stealing looks down at her shifting hem. My arm was around her shoulders, when the film broke suddenly. Our focus easily shifted in the dark from bottle dancing to lips.

It was love at first kiss, complete with skyrockets, flares, and a ride home on a magic carpet, that included a human touch in places on my body only I had known were there. Janis' touching was sensitive, wonderfully gentle, and warmly passionate.

Soon after, Janis suggested we could entertain ourselves less expensively watching TV at her house.

That first night on the couch, it wasn't long before she had unbuttoned my shirt, pulled it off, unbuckled my belt and zipped open my fly, and peeled off my pants and briefs. Leaning toward her, I opened her blouse, very slowly pulling it off her shoulders, down her arms, and away from her body. I paused in awe of my experience of her, and her glow of ecstasy. Continuing the ritual, I pulled her bra straps down over her shoulders, unfastened the back strap, let it fall limp in her lap, and embraced her.

When I was twelve, a twelve-year-old neighbor girl I was talking with in my backyard suddenly pulled her shirt off to reveal her new growing breasts. Dancing around my yard, she chanted, "Look at me, Philip, see what I got!"

Now, it was Janis, who stood and faced me bare-chested. I kissed her below her navel. She sat back down and we embraced. I lowered my lips to her right breast and suckled it. Janis moaned in pleasure. Then, she pushed me back, spread eagle, and caressed me to my moment of ecstasy. Suddenly, my shame overcame me. I became frightened, and quickly dressed.

Even later at home, after I had my wine and my Librium, the guilt didn't diminish, nor did the confusion of whether I was feeling shame or love. As Janis and I saw more of each other and our families over the following weeks and months, including the holidays, my doubts went unresolved, lost in the surface activity, the excitement of a friendship ring, and the sex. Perhaps this was the answer to all of my problems. Perhaps it was love. Maybe we should marry. It's another Tuesday night. We're alone at her house. Let's have sex!

With the spring, Janis and I enjoyed time together in the park, where we would talk about our future. I relived the pain I felt after my plans with Jackie fell through. I told Janis how I didn't want that to happen with us. She was frank as well with me about her feelings. Even when I asked her how she had learned so much about sex, she said matter-of-factly, "My brother-in-law taught me." The implications of that escaped me as I continued to be self-absorbed about my limited future as a broom pusher. Janis sensed these insecurities in me, as did her mother. As the relationship weakened over time, I would temporarily charm Janis back to me, only to lose her again in my storms of negativity.

One hot Saturday in July, the temperature on the loading dock at Koepplinger's was over 100 degrees. I had been struggling with the heat all morning. After I got home from work, Janis called.

"Jim and Winnie are going to the bar and want to double date with us."

Jim and Winnie both had Cerebral Palsy. I didn't like bars. And I certainly didn't like Jim, who I had seen at the MAC making eyes at Janis. But thinking I could put up with a couple of hours of Jim and Winnie and the bar crowd for a night with Janis, I consented. Following a long nap, I arrived at Janis's to find her more chipper than usual, and more heavily perfumed than clothed. She wore only a jet black miniskirt and a bright red see-through tubetop, that accented her breasts.

I had never seen her dressed this way in public, but she assured me, "I'm doing this for you, Philip." Something was not right about it, I felt, but I certainly was enjoying the view. Once we were on our way, Janis leaned over to me, opened my pants and lowered her head to my lap, and caressed me with her warm tongue. I slipped my right hand inside her tubetop, cupping her breast in my palm. It was almost impossible to keep my mind on driving. As Janis sat up, I kissed her bare shoulder when it passed my face. Leaning back in her seat, contentment and satisfaction on her face, I reached over, put my hand under her skirt, and felt her warm thigh.

Minutes later, as I pulled into the lot at the Country & Western bar, Jim was standing outside alone.

"Where's Winnie?" I shouted out my driver's side window.

"Oh, Winnie couldn't make it. She had to change her plans at the last minute. The three of us can still have fun. Meet you at the door."

I parked my car, buckling my belt as I walked. The wet feeling in my briefs reminded me to savor the events I'd just experienced. Watching Janis walk through the parking lot from behind, I decided the end result tonight would be worth any agony with Jim.

"What's wrong, Phil? Do you think I'm going steal Janis from you?" Jim said, smiling as our trio met at the door.

Then, he kissed Janis' bare shoulder when she walked by as he held open the door. The two exchanged winks. Something wasn't right. Inside the bar, at a table in a secluded corner, Janis sat between me and Jim. Then they ordered highballs and I ordered my Coke.

Jim cracked, "What's wrong? Can't you drink like a man, Phil?"

I was used to this kind of comment from friends at the MAC.

"I don't drink and drive, Jim." And with a glance at Janis, I added, "Besides, I want my body in working order later tonight."

I laid my hand on the inside of Janis' thigh and felt her pubic hair on the tip of my little finger. I felt in control again. How could she dump me for Jim, or anyone? But within minutes, I began to see she had planned to dump me. She nudged closer and closer to Jim. Her warm skin pulled away from my hand. Feeling frightened, lonely, and angry, I asked myself how I could be so stupid to put myself in this situation.

Angry, I blurted out, "Jim, you can't destroy in three hours what has taken me nine months to build!"

"Oh, yeah? Watch!"

Grabbing Janis and pulling her close to him, he kissed her mouth, his arms around her middle, his hands touching the soft skin surrounding her bare navel. Enraged, I tossed my Coke at Jim, but hit Janis in her belly. She let out a scream when the ice cold drink hit. As she and Jim pulled back, the table went over.

I ran out and drove home feeling desperately lonely.

I arrived at the dark and empty house and went straight for the refrigerator without turning on a light. I was on a mission to drown all thoughts of Jim enjoying Janis' erotic pleasures. After four glasses of wine and a couple Librium, nothing! The old magic wasn't working! In sheer desperation I found a bottle of Mama's whiskey and gulped down a glassful like I did my wine. It burned like nothing I had ever drank before, but, wow! I instinctively made a bee line to my bed, passing out as my head hit my pillow.

The next morning, Janis wouldn't speak to me on the phone. It was over and I knew it. After all, Jim had a good job with advancement potential in the same business as her father, and he even owned his own home, all of which pleased her parents. In less than a year, they married. Jim had won the grand prize.

Sleeping became an effort and pain gripped my body. The doctor couldn't explain my pain and my sleepless nights, but he prescribed once-a-week injections of Compazine. When the pains and the sleepless nights persisted, the doctor prescribed Dalmane and Nembutal. I had no understanding of the potential risks of drug interactions with my Librium and my wine intake, not to mention the fact that these drugs can accent depression and the very joint pains they were prescribed to diminish.

FILLING THE VOID WITH TOYS

Limited to a 4 foot by 8 foot space in the corner of the basement, I returned to model railroading using a new smaller scale called "N" gauge that was half the size of the popular "HO" scale. I had earned the trains in trade with hobby dealer, Bob Beader, who I had met while working at New Horizons. My Cerebral Palsy didn't help to handle the smaller gauge. I focused on my obsession, isolating myself, coming out of the basement only to eat, sleep and work.

One attempt I made to get back out in public was through a membership in an "N" scale club. What initially attracted my attention was a display in a local hotel lobby. The entire layout was built in 4' by 8' sections (modules). Each club member built one module to a standard that enabled each module to be connected together in the finished configuration. I knew if I could build a module to specification, I'd be taken seriously by other model railroaders.

I got a copy of the specs and set about to build a "four footer," as the modules were called. Each module had a name and told some kind a story. I called mine, "Nervous Corners." It was a small town with a freight siding and a sharp bend at the crossroads. I staged an accident in the corner. When I took it to the club house and the members saw what I could build, they were amazed. Although I became a full-fledged member, I eventually was disillusioned by the political bickering that went on like it did in every other club I had ever joined. I did learn a lot from the Society Of "N" Scalers, including how to build scenery and realistic mountains. I taught some of them the fine art of laying track and ballasting.

Another Janis?

During this same time, I returned to the MAC once in a while. It was difficult having to see Janis and Jim there on occasion pretending to be happily married. Sooner or later they would stop coming to the meetings, settle into married life, and not be seen again. I was there hoping lightning would strike again. It did. Her name was Joanna, a brunette, with a terrific figure.

As we talked, I realized Joanna was a bit more affected by Cerebral Palsy than Janis or Jackie, but I saw her as an answer to my prayers. Our first date at the movies went well. The next time, I invited her for a swim at Uncle Leo's house at the lake. When she came out in a two piece suit, my heart was throbbing. I knew Joanna was the one for me. Following the next MAC meeting, we went out for burgers and made plans for a date to the MAC's annual banquet, a real dress-up affair.

This would be the night I would take her home, get a good-night kiss in the driveway, and then go in for the kill. All that night I dreamed of one thing as I watched Joanna in her strapless gown. When the moment came in her driveway, I slid to her side of the car and we embraced. As I kissed her, I slipped one hand down her cleavage, and groped for the zipper at the back of her gown with my other hand. Anticipating the response I had gotten from Janis, instead, Joanna recoiled.

"Hey, buddy! No guy is going to get his hands on me until I have his ring on my finger!"

"All right, if that's the way you feel! I guess it'll be a cold day in hell before that happens," I said with anger, as I reached across her lap to open the door. As I did, I pulled up her skirt to plant my hand on her thigh, only to feel it slide out from under my touch as she slammed the door in my face.

Then Came Joyce

At the September MAC Meeting, I overheard a conversation about two people I knew from the CP Club, George and Joyce, and how after many years together they had just broken up. I remembered how excited I was when I first saw her, even though she belonged to another man. I also recalled the night I took Joyce, Mike, and Marion to the MAC's Valentine's

Day Party. I thought, "Why not call Joyce? Distance was no barrier now that I owned a car." I called her the next afternoon after work.

Her phone rang, and then, her voice: "Hello?"

I became suddenly nervous. "Joyce? This is Phil Schmucker. I am calling because I was thinking it might be fun to go to a movie together Tuesday night."

When she didn't immediately reply, I hung on to that silence for dear life. Somehow I found the courage to overcome my fear of rejection and I spoke again.

"I'll come over about seven and we'll take in a movie, then stop for something to eat and talk afterward."

Again, for a few seconds, nothing. Then, with just a hint of hesitation in her voice, Joyce accepted my invitation.

When Tuesday came, I didn't feel the same excitement level about a first date. Maybe I was anticipating rejection. But I had to risk it if I was ever going to meet someone and build a meaningful and lasting relationship.

I felt like I had done all of this before. The drive to my date's home. Her mother at the door. Waiting on the couch. It was as if my emotions had shifted to neutral. It was like feeling nothing. Even when Joyce came into the room: I felt no fear or anticipation. I felt nothing. It was all too automatic. Pick up the date. Go out to a movie. Stop after at a restaurant. Talk. Nothing to it. No big deal.

When I brought Joyce home around 11:30, her mother was waiting at the door to help her in. I knew this would happen. I knew I wouldn't get a kiss. But I asked for a date for the following week and she accepted.

Even our third date was predictably boring. We parked in her driveway. We got half undressed. We kissed. We fondled. We planned our next date. And that was that. No fireworks. No magic carpet ride.

Over the months, our matter-of-fact weekly movie dates, monthly MAC meetings, and occasional Adult CP meetings continued through the winter and spring, then into the summer. As the time went by, the matter-of-factness of our routine grew into something more than mere habit or convenience. A relationship developed that would change both of our lives.

It was the right time for us both. I had been thinking again of moving out on my own. So had Joyce. In fact, we had separately enrolled in a counselling program at the CP Center intended to help clients establish independence. What the Center meant by independence and what Joyce and I had in mind, which was totally taking care of ourselves, were two different things. The Center had daycare, housemaids, and other programs set up that we wanted no part of. We wanted to do our own housework and our own cooking. However, on my bakery income, I couldn't really afford to be independent. At the same time, neither Joyce nor I wanted to live like the Center's concept of a helpless model CP citizen. We were certainly radicals in our day.

The Proposal

On a Good Friday evening, after our movie date, and after we had made love in my car in her driveway, we continued to talk about our problems working with the system, and finding a way to live independently, when Joyce suggested that we live together. The concept hit me like a bolt of lightning. I actually slid back over to the driver's side of the front seat. I looked at her for several seconds before speaking.

"Don't you think we should be married before we start talking about living together?"

She just smiled. Then, it sank in. In a rush of feelings, I moved to embrace her. I kissed her passionately, then pulled back a bit.

"OK," I tried to say with male assuredness, "If you want to live with me, let's make it official. Joyce, will you marry me?"

One second. Two seconds. Three seconds ... "Yes," she said in her firm, but quiet voice.

We sat for the longest time, simply staring into each other's eyes. In the distance, the plaintive rising pitch of an early morning freight reached its peak, then slowly softened as the train rumbled into the distance.

This was so soft a feeling. Almost too quiet. Very nearly unsure. Where was the excitement and ecstasy I thought I was supposed to be feeling? This is Easter weekend! My entire family will be home. Surely, they'll celebrate my good news, just like we did when Michael, Linda and Laurie announced their engagements.

"Great!" I thought when I saw the lights were on. Ma was up watching the late, late movie. John was probably watching the same movie down in the basement. Even before I could get through the kitchen and into the family room, I shouted.

"Ma, I'm going to marry Joyce!"

"Be still, I can't hear the TV."

Closer now, I shouted again.

"Ma! I'm going to marry Joyce!"

Without much of a stir, Mama half-turned in her seat to look back at me over her shoulder just as a commercial began, "That's nice, dear."

"Nice?"

With that, I wheeled around and headed straight for the refrigerator and my wine. I unscrewed the cap and drank it down like it was soda pop.

Mama's voice from the family room said, "You going to drink like that when you're married?"

"Who the hell cares?" I asked the darkness.

I headed off to my room to crash, but woke minutes later to screaming coming from the basement.

"What the hell's the matter with you, Lorraine? How in sam hell are the two of them going to get married and live by themselves? What's he going to do? Bring his damn bride *here* to live?"

As the screaming match continued, I wobbled back into the kitchen and gulped a full glass of Mama's whiskey, which was sitting out on the counter, hoping that would knock me out. I wondered what kind of reception Joyce's news had received from her family? What I discovered later on was that it was *also* negative, though not as crudely so.

Rings And Things

With the engagement on, it was time to buy the set of rings. Isn't this what every engaged couple does? It's the nature of things. So, the week after Easter, I took Joyce to the mall to shop for rings. The mall really stretched our comfort zones with its large parking lot, all the walking, the crowds, the doors that are difficult to open. But here we were at the mall, walking into a jewelry store. We walked to the counter displaying the wedding rings. We stood. We waited. No salesperson. There were no other customers in the store at the time, so I figured we were clearly being ignored. I spoke up…loudly.

"Does anyone want to make some money tonight by selling some wedding rings?"

"Yes, sir," the salesperson said in an apologetic voice as he walked over to us.

When he pulled out a tray of rings from the counter, I was shocked when Joyce said, "I don't want a diamond. I'm too old for that stuff. That stuff is for younger women."

I never expected Joyce would prefer a plain wedding band. I felt like I was cheating her. Wasn't my bride supposed to have a diamond? It was certainly a part of my dream! But it was not her dream.

The next challenge was to locate a place to live. Joyce and I started working together with the counselors at the CP Center. They only offered us listings for apartments in new Senior high-rises with handicap-accessible features in the inner city. My dream was a home with a full basement for my model railroad and a two-car garage, where I could park on one side and rebuild my Santa's Toy Shop on the other side.

On my days off, Joyce and I looked at the apartments the Center referred us to. They were mostly one bedroom units, with no room to build anything. Too far from stores. No nearby churches. The grounds seemed safe, but what about the surrounding streets and neighborhoods? Joyce and I shared these feelings, as did her mother. Ma said nothing.

Finally, one morning at the bakery, Bob, the mechanic, told me about a place.

"It's out in Roseville. It's a townhouse co-op. And they have full basements. You ought to drive out there and take a look."

I took Joyce out there the next day. And we were both pleased with the place. It was a huge complex. The Manager showed us the two bedroom unit with the full basement. There was even a patch of lawn in front that I didn't have to cut.

On the promise that we'd have a two bedroom unit by June, I signed a lease for a one bedroom unit for this December. Our plan was that I'd move in and set up housekeeping, transfer into the two bedroom unit in June, when Joyce would move in, and then in July, we'd marry.

My moving day was the day after Christmas. It was cold and snowing heavily. I had to work that day, so in the morning John and Laurie's husband moved my things into the townhouse. I found my things thrown inside the door, including soggy bed linens, which they had dropped in the snow. I called Mama, and that night she drove herself 45 miles to help me make some sense of the situation. We put the bed together and arranged furniture.

STILL A FRIGHTENED CHILD

The first few months were a hellish experience for me. At night, I jumped at every little sound. The neighbors sounded like they were in the next room. The winter was severe, making it hard getting to and from work, as well as adding to the sense of isolation once I got home. In fact, the mini-series, Roots, was on TV. On the way home from the bakery, I'd stock up on wine and spend my nights watching the series and drinking my wine.

Nothing seemed to be going the way I thought it should. My wedding plans didn't make me feel any better about myself. Work certainly didn't boost my spirits. And my drinking seemed to be affecting my relationships at the railroader club, as well. I kept thinking things would change when Joyce and I were together.

In the meantime, even Joyce saw the changes in me since our engagement. She certainly didn't like the way Mama treated me or how I became a ten-year-old child at Mama's house. In fact, Joyce and her mother were caught off guard by our "family ways" one Sunday at our townhouse as they planned the wedding shower with Ma. It was the first time the two mothers had met, and so a lot of the talk was about family on both sides.

The conversation turned to questions about Daddy. I had gone to my room to get the only picture of Daddy I had and handed it to Joyce's mother.

"He was quite a handsome man," she said, sharing it with Joyce. Joyce nodded.

Without warning, Mama shouted, "Damn you, Philip! Stop putting your father on a pedestal! He wasn't that great a man. Furthermore, you are not getting any money from your uncles, just your sisters. You have your share." Joyce and her mother looked at each other, utterly confused. It sure didn't have anything to do with planning Joyce's shower.

As it turned out, the shower was an experience in itself that Joyce's family would remember for a long time. One of my mother's more notable quotes of the day, as reported to us by Joyce's sister, was "My son deserves a real wedding, just like anyone else."

When the big week arrived, Joyce and I were ready, though I began to worry that it would be nothing like I had dreamed it would be, and that the whole thing would be another major disappointment. Things began to unravel Wednesday, when my best man, Rusty, backed out. I hung up the phone in a panic. Thursday is the rehearsal and I have no best man! What could I tell Joyce? I went to the kitchen and drank wine until I passed out.

When I woke later that evening, I called Mama, but I was still too drunk to be consoled. More than anything, I was fearful of being embarrassed in front of Joyce, her family and our friends. I lost control. I felt as if my life was shattering. I wanted to die. I poured myself a large glass of wine and swallowed almost 70 10mg capsules of Librium. I called Mama again and told her what I had done, but remembering that Dr. Ryan had told her that Librium cannot kill, she did nothing. She thought this was just another one of my drunks.

The next morning she tried calling, but got no answer. When she went to work, and found I wasn't a the bakery, she left work and drove to my place. She found my door unlocked, and me passed out on my bed fully dressed. She tried to wake me.

"Philip! Philip! Wake up, dammit!"

She shook me violently.

"Goddamn you, Philip! Wake up! Wake up!"

No response. She went to the kitchen and started a pot of coffee. Then she filled the tub with cold water, came back into my room, stripped me naked, and dragged me into the cold bath.

"Come on, you son-of-a-bitch! You have a wedding rehearsal tonight! Wake up! Get a grip on yourself, dammit!"

As I came to, she wrapped my robe around me, then walked me into the kitchen and poured several cups of black coffee into me.

When Mama phoned Joyce and her mother to tell them what had happened, they were perplexed. Their first thought was to postpone the wedding. They even asked the minister's advice. But as far as Mama was concerned, this wedding was going to happen come sunshine or Armageddon. The minister agreed. Why postpone a wedding just because I wanted to die at the time and happened to be just a little groggy?

Between me and Mama, Joyce was so stressed out she didn't know which way was which. She loved me very much. She felt I needed her support, and the sooner the wedding, the sooner she could be with me and stand by me.

Where was I in all of this? I had all I could do to deal with a tremendous hangover the morning of the wedding. I had had little sleep and nothing to eat for over 24 hours. I dressed in my usual shirt and slacks, then put on my new sport coat. (I only wore a tux in my dreams.) In the mirror I said to myself, "This is it, fella. After you are married everything will work out. You'll see. You'll live and love forever." With a wink from my optimistic self, I drove my hangover to Mama's house.

Mama was entertaining guests in the living room before the wedding, when I walked in.

"Well, where the hell have you been? I got all this work to do getting this damn place ready for your wedding!"

With the help of a drink or two, by late afternoon she calmed down. I had a chance to eat some solid food.

The church ceremony was a circus. No one knew what they were doing, including myself. Everyone seemed to be running in circles. My cousin Gordon stepped in at the last minute as Best Man. The minister was forty-five minutes late! As the music began, Joyce's brother escorted her down the aisle. I could see Joyce was trembling. At the altar steps, I took her arm, and we climbed the three steps to two overstuffed chairs.

It was then that I noticed the minister's hands. He was supposed to have the rings on one of his pinky fingers. No rings! As we knelt at the rail for the vows, all I could think about were the rings. When the minister felt his hand for Joyce's ring, he went for his own wedding band, which wouldn't budge. Suddenly it popped over his knuckle, and he continued with the ceremony. When I placed the huge ring on her hand, Joyce was utterly confused. The minister's band was big enough to go around two of her fingers. After the ceremony, Gordon retrieved our bands from the minister's office.

Ma had prepared our reception. While my family gathered in the basement where the booze was, Joyce's family remained up in the family room, and our friends visited in the living room. Of all of our friends with Cerebral Palsy, only Marian and her new husband, Bob, came to help us celebrate, and they left early without saying good-bye.

We left Mama's at a respectable time to begin our honeymoon, which we decided would be during a four-day convention in Columbus, Ohio, of a handicap lobbying group of which we were members. We went back to our townhouse for the night, so we could leave for the convention the next morning.

At our home, I made my nightly dash to the refrigerator for my wine. Joyce went up to the bedroom to prepare for her wedding night. It was an hour before I joined her in our bed.

As I crawled under the covers, I said, "Honey, let's wait a while." That "while" grew into days.

Honeymoon

My biggest dream was a reality. I was married. Now I was about to begin my honeymoon. But I was still a scared little boy. Strangely, we ate our first breakfast, packed up the car, and headed out on the road like two people who had been married for years! After one stop at Joyce's sister's, we were headed for Columbus. We arrived early afternoon, registered, and went up to our room for a well-deserved nap. That evening, we attended one of the workshops. It was about handicapped people needing to band together to make our demands heard.

"But why do we always have to demand?" I kept asking myself. "Why can't we just do it ourselves?"

After the workshop, we returned to our room. Joyce waited for me in bed, while I enjoyed a few glasses of wine, still afraid to consummate our marriage. With all of my sexual adventures, intercourse was something I had never attempted. I was too afraid.

The next morning, after breakfast, Joyce went with some of her friends to shop in the mall across from the hotel. On my own, I found a hobby shop nearby, where I spent the morning alone. On the way back to the hotel, I checked on my car, my lifeline! When I spotted oil on the pavement, all I could imagine was the worst.

"Oh, my God, now what! We'll have to return home in the morning!"

Joyce was terribly disappointed. But I insisted that we check out first thing after breakfast. We left the convention two days early, saying goodbye to no one. Our honeymoon was over. We drove home in silence, each wondering in our hearts about the future, and feeling that what was happening wasn't what married life is supposed to be like. Was it?

I believed everything could be fixed. I was convinced it would all work out. If I only knew how!

9

this is marriage?

Within a few short weeks, we knew there was something very wrong with our relationship. Following old patterns, I retreated to the basement and became a recluse like I was at Mama's. Living the fantasy also eluded Joyce, though she tried to use her housekeeping role to justify herself. Our lives quickly turned into deadly routine. Joyce began her day doing repeated cleaning. Then she had lunch. Following lunch, she watched soap operas. When I came home from my dead-end half day at the bakery, I headed straight for my jug of wine in the fridge, slug down two glassfuls, then stagger to bed for a nap.

After Joyce's soaps, she joined me in bed, waking me from my nap. Still groggy from my wine, we made our flustered attempt at having sex. Then I retreated to my basement sanctuary. Seemingly happy, Joyce prepared dinner. After we ate, I returned to my trains until 11, when I would force myself to break away, drink more wine, then stagger up to bed. Each day, the same scenario. I had trapped myself in old patterns, dooming our marriage from the start.

Sundays, we made our trip to church, hoping to find answers, any answer, to questions like: Where was the peace and love we had expected from married life?

ALCOHOLICS ANONYMOUS

By the end of our first year of marital non-bliss, my drinking had dramatically increased. I looked to our church, counselling, the CP Center, and family, but I found no easy answers. I had known of Alcoholics Anonymous because a couple of my uncles attended meetings and had stopped drinking. I was not sure what A.A. was all about, but I knew I had to do something and do it fast. My life couldn't go on this way. My biggest motivation was to make my marriage work.

One hot Tuesday evening in June, Joyce and I watched TV together. Even as I would spend time with her, I would drink steadily. That night I knew what I had to do. When I poured the last drop from the jug, I said, "That's it! I better go to A.A. tomorrow." Joyce said nothing.

Wednesday morning I called A.A. to find a meeting. There was one right in the neighborhood about a mile away. After supper, I bathed and dressed for the meeting. The idea of meeting with strangers always frightened me. Talking with strangers about my drinking problems scared me even more. However, the members welcomed me with open arms. It reminded me of the night as a boy I had been welcomed at the Boy Scouts. After the hour-or-so meeting, I felt better about myself. Not only was I pleased with this first step, but for the first time I saw how changing me could help save my marriage.

When I came back home, I wanted to share some intimate time with Joyce, but she refused.

"Not after you've been with those drunken bums!"

I had wanted love and compassion. Instead, I was greeted with anger and resentment. I sat on the sofa trying to explain what A.A. was all about, but Joyce would have nothing to do with it. That old terror resurfaced and I now had no relief from feeling my pain and stress in the 'fridge.

After meeting once a week for several weeks, I asked some of the members what the problem could be. They asked me how often I used to drink.

"Every night," I said.

"If you drank every night, how do you expect A.A. to work if you go to one meeting a week?"

I had no answer for that. The next evening I went to a second meeting, eventually building up to seven or eight a week. Surprisingly, Joyce reluctantly agreed to attend Alanon meetings, a support group for spouses and family of alcoholics, but all that did was feed her resentment toward the recovery concept. She never bought the idea that my problems were due to alcohol.

THE LIBRIUM

I was consistently attending seven A.A. meetings a week. Still nothing in my life was improving, other than the fact that I had stopped drinking. Then it hit me. Could my continued problems have anything to do with taking the Librium? After a year in A.A., I understood I had to be "rigorously" honest with myself. Quality sobriety had to include getting off the Librium, too. I had to be totally clean, and I knew it wouldn't be easy. Experience had proven to me there was no going cold turkey off this stuff.

Through a drug abuse counsellor I knew in A.A., I went to a detox center. During the intake interview with the doctor, I said I had been taking Librium for seventeen years. The doctor could hardly believe it. He had never heard of a person taking Librium that long and at that high a dosage level!

The program was four weeks of hell. After the first week of detox, I could do nothing for myself. I couldn't even feed myself. The unusual factors of the Cerebral Palsy and the Librium withdrawals did a real number on my body. One night during the second week, my blood pressure went through the roof, and I thought I was going to die. The staff thought they might lose me, too.

I knew Joyce had strong feelings about me, my family, and why I was who I was, but I didn't begin to understand what she was feeling until the one time Mama brought Joyce and her mother to visit me during treatment. That same day my A.A. sponsor, Bill, showed up, for a visit.

I watched Joyce's resentment toward this man overwhelm her as Bill (and A.A.) literally stepped in between me, Joyce, Mama, and even the treatment center staff. While the world had its ideas of what I needed, there was only one sure way, the A.A. way. During the visit, which Bill dominated, Joyce saw how I bought into Bill and his "program" for me. Joyce saw how I had traded one dependency for another, and it angered her that her needs and our marriage had been discounted by Bill.

One evening after returning from the treatment center, I wanted to spend a romantic evening with Joyce. I called Bill to let him know I wouldn't be at the meeting.

"Hi, Bill. I've decided Joyce and I need some romance tonight. So, I won't be at the meeting."

"What! I thought you wanted sobriety? Staying home playing kissie face with Joyce isn't where you'll find sobriety!"

"But Joyce needs me! We have to work on our relationship."

"Phil, you have to work on Phil."

"But ..."

"No buts! If you want to be alive to even *think* about having a relationship in your life that you can contribute to, you must do as I tell you. You have to work on Phil. Joyce will have to wait."

"Well, if you say so."

"I say so. Now, get your ass over here and we'll go to the meeting."

During the conversation, I watched Joyce's face fall with disappointment, then tighten with anger. I couldn't look at her as I said good-bye and went out the door. A voice in me told me to stay, but Bill had firmly planted the message in me and I kept heading out to the car.

That night was the turning point in our marriage. Joyce dropped out of Alanon. I knew she couldn't support me in A.A., but I didn't appreciate the anger of some of the Alanon members who I overheard telling her, "Divorce the son-of-a-bitch! He'll *never* get better. Why, someday he might even kill you!" With advice like that from Alanon members, it was better she not go.

THE END OF MARRIAGE

After eighteen months of sobriety, including six months of Librium-free existence, my metabolism was still undergoing major changes. I was feeling hot and cold at the same time. I had never perspired the way I did now. When I called the treatment center, no one could tell me what the long-term withdrawal from Librium would be like.

One cold and rainy spring afternoon when I came home from work, I was on the edge of insanity. Joyce was busy vacuuming as she did everyday.

"Honey, would you move the couch, so I can clean under it?" she asked.

"Joyce, you just vacuumed under it yesterday, and the day before, and the day before that. It's too heavy for me to move."

"Oh, now you're calling me a slob!" she shot back.

"No! Joyce! You always twist my words around! Stop doing that!"

With that, I decided I had to do something more for myself. This hell Joyce and I were living had to stop. Joyce had already decided to seek therapy for herself. I was pleased when she told me her decision. She was seeing a therapist at the county center once a week, taking dial-a-ride to get there and back.

I decided I needed to do something about my withdrawal symptoms, so I called a nearby drug counselling center, which referred me to Steve Campbell, a well-known therapist in the area, whose colleagues called him "The Miracle Worker." I could hardly wait to get off the phone with his office to tell Joyce. However, when I told her where his office was located, it turned out to be in the same building where her therapist was located.

Joyce flew into a rage, accusing me of spying on her. She went for my hair, pulling it, and in defending myself by trying to push her away, we got into the worse scrap we ever had. The yelling and screaming was dreadful. I finally got away from her and escaped into the basement. Eventually all quieted down. Joyce started supper, while I took out my frustrations on my trains.

I wanted to talk with Bill. He was my only relief valve. I knew he wouldn't be home from work, yet. Tonight was our weekly A.A. meeting in Windsor. I tried not to think about the fight with Joyce, or how hungry, angry, lonely or tired I felt. At 4, when Joyce called me for supper, I froze with fear. All of my emotions were welling up in me. The more I thought about facing her, the more frozen I felt. My compulsion was to run, but I was trapped in the basement. I kept yelling up, "In a minute. In a minute." I knew Joyce would be angry. Like a cornered animal, I waited. Suppertime passed. Soon it would be time to leave for the A.A. meeting.

Somehow, when the time came, I found the strength to come up and face her anger. Again, she went for my hair and another fight started. Too late for flight, now it was time to fight. I lost control for a moment and wanted to kill her. I knew if I touched her, I would. That feeling frightened me. I backed off and cried to her and anyone else in the universe for help. I didn't want to live like this way any longer! Joyce was frightened by the hatred and the panic in my eyes, and ran to the neighbor's. I called the police on our phone, because I didn't know what else to do to get help.

The police offered to take me to a hospital. I thought that would be a good idea. Joyce came home after calling her brother from the neighbor's phone. After he arrived, we all left for the hospital. Joyce and her brother followed me in the police car. When I noticed the officer had turned the opposite way from the local hospital, I pleaded, "Where are you taking me?"

"Where the hell did you think you were going?" the officer said, "Clinton Valley Psychiatric."

I collapsed in the back seat with, "Oh, God! No!"

At the hospital, Joyce and I were separately and intensely interrogated. The staff convinced me to commit myself. By doing so, I could sign myself out in three days. If I hadn't signed myself in, I faced a court-ordered sixty days of confinement. I signed the papers and was immediately processed into a ward. Once inside, I became uncooperative and was threatened by the attendant with padded cell confinement. It didn't matter. I wanted to die, anyway. When I continued to resist, he took me down the corridor and left me alone in the unlocked cell to ponder my choice. I cried like a baby.

My mind picked a parallel moment that had been buried all these years. Doctor Days, we called them in school. I feared them. Once a year, an attendant at our special school came to each classroom with a list. Children on the list were to be examined by the doctor. I cringed as the list was read until the attendant passed the "S's." Only then would my fear subside. The other students would snicker, knowing what fate lay ahead for the "chosen ones."

One year when my name came up, we were led to the clinic and into a locker room like the condemned children we already were. Boys were given a diaper with two safety pins, and told to undress completely. Girls were given two diapers and four pins, one diaper for the bottom and one for whatever they needed to cover on top. Students who required help or who refused were helped by the attendant. The attendant was usually a female nurse, but a male attendant sometimes was available for the boys. Not always. I hated this entire process, and would pretend to be sick to avoid it, but the nurses always saw through my charade. I would be forcibly stripped and the diaper crudely pinned on me.

Wrapped in paper robes, the boys and the girls were brought together in the clinic waiting room. Many times our diapers would fall off our bodies before we got to the waiting area, causing painful embarrassment. The older teenagers appeared to enjoy all of this, and even took advantage of the poor supervision. Some of the teenagers' diapers fell off. A few teens flashed the younger ones, frightening us. Other teens fondled one another.

When my name was called, I went into the clinic's examination room. I felt like a condemned prisoner walking to my crucifixion. A nurse removed my paper robe and my diaper, and I stood cold and naked in front of the doctor and the staff. I felt terribly ashamed. Then I was told to walk back and forth. As the doctor rambled on in medical talk, one of the nurses made notes. Next, I was lifted onto a table, where the doctor pulled at my arms and legs and stretched them to sometimes painful extremes. Lastly, I was sat up at the edge of the table with my legs hanging over the side. The doctor spread my knees as far apart as they would go, causing excruciating pain, not to mention more humiliation. Wearing no diaper and with very little of the paper robe left to cover myself, I was sent back to the locker room to dress.

I remembered complaining to Mama at the time, but all she would say was, "The people at school are doing this for your own good. They know what's good for you. They know what they are doing."

Of course, when I became a teenager, I, too, made the most of the experience, especially when one of the girls would take her diaper off her breasts. I didn't understand why I enjoyed it, but the play helped take the edge off of the embarrassment I knew awaited me in the examining room.

The hospital attendant's voice broke my reverie.

"Are you going to cooperate now?"

In a less than audible voice, I whimpered, "Yes."

He helped me to my feet and returned me to the ward.

The next morning, when it came time to take my drugs at the drug station, I protested. I had no doubt that the Librium, Nembutol and everything else, including the alcohol, had combined to bring me to this point. I didn't want to put any more drugs in my body.

"That shit is what brought me here in the first place!"

"Take it or else!" the attendant said.

I stood my ground and again was taken to the small, solitary cell. Several minutes later, the attendant returned with the drug. When I relented and took the stuff, he brought me to the Day Room, where I was given water colors. I painted a landscape of my large dream house, where I would someday live with a loving and committed spouse.

After enduring three days of that hell hole, I signed myself out. Mama and Aunt Mary picked me up.

BACK HOME AGAIN

It was obvious the moment I arrived home that Joyce had moved out. Most of the linens and the appliances were gone. Strangely, she left behind all of her precious cookbooks. I tossed my painting of our dream home into my circular file. It was painful being alone, my dream of a marriage so unceremoniously ended. I did have my job at the bakery, so I knew I could make a life for myself. Content for the moment with what I had, I attended an A.A. meeting that first night.

My contentment dissolved into fantasy over the next six months, as I dreamed of reestablishing my marriage with Joyce. I made numerous attempts to get through to her. One day, while I was in the locker room of the bakery, ready to enjoy a refreshing shower before going home, a stranger walked up behind me.

"Are you Philip Schmucker?"

"Yes?"

"Greetings!" he said as he slapped a divorce subpoena into my hand.

The shock was more than I could handle. It was all I could do to dress. I wanted to die. I thought of picking up a jug of wine, but I knew that wasn't an option. Instead, I stopped at John's house. An A.A. buddy, John saw this day coming for me for many weeks. He went through the same terror a few years before. We had been talking for several hours when I realized I was avoiding the inevitable and must return to my empty town house. I had to accept the fact that the possibility of Joyce coming home to me was gone. I hung on to nearly three years of sobriety for dear life, and managed to find a lawyer to handle my end of the divorce without having to appear in court myself. He obtained a simple judgment the following October stating that each of us could keep what was ours.

LIFE GOES ON

I began therapy with Steve Campbell the week after returning from the hospital. During the first appointment, while trying to show Steve some of the frustrations I had to deal with, I broke his telephone. Steve saw a challenge in me he couldn't pass up.

He told me in so many words, "If there is a kind, caring, loving, and lovable man buried in this shell of humanity, I'll help you find it."

We began work the following week, launching a steady five-year relationship, which continued on a part-time basis for another three years after that. Much of our work was done in group and focused on what Steve called "little work," by which he meant re-parenting, based on the transactional analysis theories of Eric Berne and Max Steiner.

During one session held in his home, a bus skidded into several parked cars in front of his home, including mine. The noise disrupted the group. As I bolted out of his door in a typical panic, Steve was right behind me, step for step, yelling, "Think! Think! Think! Think!" I stopped halfway out to the street and turned, realizing I had been out of control and now I was back in control.

"I couldn't have asked for a better opportunity to help you realize what you have been doing to yourself! I just didn't know how long it would take to stick!" he huffed excitedly.

Clearly, Steve Campbell was the first person to see what had happened to me. He saw how my frustrations were shaped by the negative events in my life. He saw how my father's inability to accept my disability was passed on to me in perfectionism, judging others, self-destructive anger, and incapacitating fears and obsessions. Many of my issues would send Steve back to his own teachers, saying he had never encountered a person as beaten and bruised as me.

The work with Steve also helped me find gratitude for what I did have. I began to put more effort into my menial job at the bakery. I realized that whatever I did in life, to do it to the best of my ability. I was thankful I had my job to help keep me busy. I was thankful I was sober. On the other hand, my marriage vow before God remained an issue. The marriage may have ended in the eyes of the world, but deep inside I felt I had to reconcile this with God and rebuild the relationship.

Eighteen months after my divorce, as I was punching in one cold November morning, some of the men gathered around me to tell me about a rumor of a massive layoff. Fifty employees were to be cut, they said. Since Mama had retired, management had changed and it seemed the business had also changed. Now, Keopplinger's had lost a contract with a big food chain. First thing at 8 a.m., Don called me into his office to tell me I had been laid off! It was a shock worse than my divorce.

"Oh God," I thought, "Can You hate me this much, You take my job away, too?"

On the way home, I bought a jug of wine, then stopped at John's house. When John later told Bill I was drinking again, Bill dropped me. I didn't think A.A. sponsors operated that way, but I didn't much care. The rejection from the bakery was worse.

Three days after the layoff, Mama drove me to the union hall since I was in no condition to drive myself. I expected to see the other forty-nine men who were laid off, but to my consternation, I discovered I was the only one laid off! It was all a scam by the new management to fire me and make it look like a layoff.

It wasn't long after that my minister called me into his office. It seemed someone was giving me a hundred dollars every week, which Pastor Alwerdt would dole out to me. It wasn't until he wrote the last check that he let the cat out of the bag.

"Well, now I can tell John you got the whole amount of a thousand dollars," he said, signing the check.

"John, who?" I asked. "John Mather?"

When he nodded, I became furious. It was guilt money from Koepplinger! John Mather was a young executive who worked at Stroh brewery and was married to Mrs. Koepplinger's niece. When Ray Koepplinger retired, Anna sought someone with family ties and with tough executive ability to run the business. With Ray out of the way and Mama retired, John was free to dismiss me in the name of productivity. The man knew he did something wrong and he was buying me off. By cleverly giving me money through my church, I would still be able to collect unemployment at the same time.

When I consulted a lawyer, I was told what John did was certainly illegal, but I had waited too long to file suit.

"You waited one week too long. Too bad, because you could have sued the bakery and lived comfortably the rest of your life off the proceeds."

A Last Attempt At Employment

I had lost my wife, my job and my sobriety. Now I had to begin a new life with my talents and my determination to find my reason for being. Rehabilitation Services placed me in a job club, where I learned techniques to find a job. I became skilled at selling myself over the telephone. One day I successfully sold myself to a prospective employer who owned a print shop.

His response was, "Philip, you come to my shop. Show me what you say you can do, and you've got the job."

It took me fifteen minutes to drive to the print shop, but when I walked into the man's office, he told me the job had just been filled! I was humiliated standing there in this strange place, among all these strangers, everyone knowing what had just happened. Once he saw me in person, all bets were off. It was a first-class case of discrimination. I made up my mind then and there that this would be the last time anyone would do this to me. No more employment for me. I had to make it in life on my own doing something I could create for myself.

Have You Got Any Toy Trains For Sale?

There's a saying, "You can't go back." Looking at what I did to make money over the past twenty years, I saw no way of returning to any business I once had. I began living from day to day, killing time by visiting friends who owned hobby shops during the day and going to A.A. meetings at night. Every couple of weeks, I'd go on a binge. Not exactly a banner existence.

October of that year, I went to a local train show to kill a Sunday afternoon. Train shows started out as small swap meets. Over the years, they grew into a large underground black market, cutting into the retail hobby business. There in the mist of all the hustle and bustle, I got an idea. "Why can't I do this?" It was no nickel and dime stuff. Big bucks were changing hands.

The next day I went to Bob Beader's Models and Hobby on Woodward, south of Nine Mile Road in Ferndale, where my friend Dee worked. Dee had a lot of retail hobby experience working with Bob and having had her own shop at one time. She had also been my surrogate mother over the last few years. I could talk to her about things I could never discuss with Mama. Dee also encouraged me to pursue my dreams and meet life's frustrations head on.

"Good morning. What brings you here so early in the day?" she asked.

"I spent yesterday at the train show watching all those guys making tons of money selling toy trains. I think I could make some money selling toy trains that way, too," I said, as I leaned against the counter and watched Dee with her busy work.

"Great! I think you could make good money doing that," Dee agreed in her always upbeat and cheerful voice.

"Tell me, how do those guys get all that new stuff?"

"That new 'stuff' is what Bob calls 'back door' Lionel, because it comes out the back door of the factory faster than it's shipped from the loading dock. Meaning, most of that stuff is hot! Actually, Phil, you could find plenty of good merchandise at garage sales. Garage sale stuff sells faster than all that new stuff put together."

"So, how do I find garage sales?" I asked, becoming more excited by the minute.

"You get a newspaper, look them up, and go, go, go!"

I left the hobby shop soon after, more enthused about my prospects for success than I had been about anything in a long time.

Beginners Luck

The next morning, a steady chilly rain was coming down. I went to the donut shop for coffee and donuts. There I bought a paper and looked for garage sales. I found only a handful of ads. I soon discovered I needed more than the newspaper ads. I was going to need some street maps to find the streets. After a detour to a gas station for maps, I found my first garage sale. I looked around as the dampness cut through my body. I saw nothing but junk. No toy trains.

As I turned to walk back to my car, a voice inside of me said, "Ask for toy trains." I turned back to the woman, who was finishing up with another customer.

"Have ya got any toy trains?" I asked.

The woman hesitated, looking puzzled. Then, she said, "Wait a minute, I think I do." She went into the house and shortly returned with a box of trains. I looked through the box, having no idea what I was looking at.

"How much do you want for them?"

"Forty dollars," she replied.

Again, the voice inside spoke up and told me to offer less.

"Twenty," I said flatly.

"Thirty," she returned.

"OK, I'll take them."

I pulled out the thirty dollars and the woman carried the box of trains to my car and put it the back seat. I jumped in and drove triumphantly back to the hobby shop to show Dee my find. Dee slowly took the pieces out of the box one by one, exclaiming, "Oh, Phil! What a find! This is great stuff!" All I saw was broken junk. Nothing like what I saw at the show the Sunday before.

"What did you pay?" Dee asked.

"Thirty," I sheepishly replied, thinking I overpaid.

"Man, a good buy! There's about seventy-five dollars worth here. I'll make some price tags for you."

Dee helped me price the trains. The total in the box came to over seventy dollars. The next step was to find a train show to sell them at. On Dee's bulletin board was a flyer for a show in Toledo the following Sunday. Back home with my box of gold, I mustered the strength to make the phone call to reserve a table.

That next Sunday, I was off to the show. Highway driving was one of my favorite things to do. I had no problem finding the fair grounds where the train show was being held. However, parking was a fear that haunted me. I went inside, apprehensive and anxious, and waited in line for my table assignment. Then, I walked back out to my car and carried in my one box of junk. I didn't even know what to do next. Looking around to see what everyone else did, I began to put my engines and cars out on the table on their sides. I was soon ready for business.

With little to set up, I had time to walk around watching other people set up their tables. I compared my merchandise to theirs, wondering if anyone would buy my stuff. As the crowd filtered through the exhibit hall to my table, my apprehension jumped into high gear. My critical inner voice was condemning this whole idea. "Who in their right mind would buy this junk?" it kept complaining. When people began to stop and look, I felt excited. When they slowly walked away, I felt rejected. "See!" that voice nudged within me.

As an elderly man stopped and picked up one of the two engines I had, he said, "Mmm, I've been looking for one like this for a long time. Does it run?"

"It ran the last time I checked it out!" I said.

When the man set it down and moved on, my heart dropped. The negative thoughts filtered through my mind until another man came up to my table. He picked up one of the OH train cars and simply said, "I want this car. How much?"

"Two," I replied.

The man handed me two dollars and took the car! A half hour later, the first man returned.

"Boy, I sure do want that engine."

Picking it up again and examining it, he said, "Forty is a little steep. Would you take twenty?"

I said, "Thirty," wishing I hadn't.

"Well, OK. Thirty it is," as he reached into his pocket and pulled out a wad of folded bills, handing me a twenty and a ten. With that sale, I had recouped my entire investment. My fears and apprehensions lifted like a spring morning fog. Shortly after that sale, another man stopped and picked up the second engine along with a few freight cars.

"How much?"

"Ah, the engine and two cars. I'd say about fifty."

"Thirty five," he came back.

"Forty."

"Man, you sure drive a hard bargain," he smiled. "OK, I'll give you forty for the three pieces."

Three p.m. came fast. The number of customers had dwindled and other dealers were packing up for the day, even though there were two more hours for the show to run. Taking my cue, I decided to pack up, as well. Why not? I was sixty dollars richer than when I started out in the morning. I was feeling like a millionaire!

When I stopped for something to eat, I felt free and fully human for the first time in a long, long time. Here I was, eating in a restaurant and not caring when people stared at me! With a full stomach, I left the restaurant and drove home, dreaming my dream of owning my own hobby shop. Selling toy trains was the closest I had ever come to living that dream.

That winter stayed relatively warm, making my rounds of garage sales easy to accomplish. I was finding toy trains on a regular basis, nearly one a week. In addition, I placed ads in the papers and signs in stores. I made a full-time business of it. The money added up like no other business venture before. I even found an original Erector Set for seventy five dollars, which Dee helped me sell for four hundred!

At the peak of my business, I was doing thirty-five shows a year. I even saved enough money to buy myself the new VW Jetta Diesel I always wanted. It was as if I had found my niche in life. So I thought

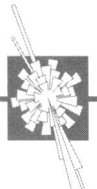

James, God's butler, completes the last page, seated in God's overstuffed chair at God's desk.

"James?"

"Sir?"

"Your observations, James."

"Sir ..." he pauses.

All Knowledge descends from the library steps with a dusty old hand bound volume in-hand. He waits.

"Floundering is the word, Sir."

"Yes."

"It's all I can think of. Floundering. The man is adrift. The sea is carrying him whichever way. The waves carry him up to incredible heights. Like a ship adrift, the waves drop out from beneath. And he…"

"Flounders, James?"

"Exactly, Sir."

God pages through the volume and smiles.

"Did you play with a toy train when you were little, James?"

"You know I did, Sir. Round and round and round that little steamer went on its clackety tracks." James allows himself a crooked smile.

"A steamer! Quite a collector's prize these days."

"Before electricity, Sir. Ran like a jewel."

"Looking through these collector's catalogs, I can see the attraction Phil has for trains. They are superb little machines. Just the thing to help develop a little boy's imagination."

"Intriguing to the little boy in men, as well, as I have read, Sir." James rises and God moves toward the desk with the bound volume of toy train catalogs.

"As our friend Phil grabs at any flotsam and jetsam that sail by on the waves as he flounders, as you poetically put it, James, he reaches for what he recognizes. It is the pull of the distant whistle. The powerful machine that can take you across continents far from your own problems, perhaps. Or better, toward your ultimate fate."

"Fate, Sir? Not a concept I've heard you discuss."

"Escape. Adventure. And, yes, fate in human terms. As if I or some other power in the universe like a planet or a star or a spirit or a shaman or a witch casts a spell and grants a wish."

"I see, Sir."

"A toy train is a wonderfully powerful icon for a child, but like all things earthly, it becomes denominated in dollars by the adult and is encased or enshrined instead of performing its marvelous magic."

"Sir?"

"Our man Phil. The toy train threads his past and future. In his basement are the ghosts of Christmas past. In his halls are boxes of Christmases present, so to speak. As he garage sales, he finds the ghosts of Christmases to come."

"There *were* trains in Dickens' time."

"The toy train is what carries his child into the future. As Phil develops his antique train business, though he avoids the old ghosts associated with his basement layout, his inner child thrives. Nothing more. It's at once simple and profound."

"I'm not sure ..."

"Metaphor, James."

"When something is likened to something else, Sir?" "That would be a simile, James. In context, a metaphor *IS* both itself and the symbol. It is an icon. In this case, there is nothing but a toy train transporting Phil's baggage through time."

"Is that sufficient, Sir?"

God steps out of the way and gestures James to be seated and to resume his reading of the transcriptions.

"Read on, James. Read on."

the toy train business changes

When Richard Kughn, Detroit businessman and owner of the world's largest Lionel collection, bought Lionel, he began a media campaign to make the public aware of the pleasure and value of old toy trains sitting in their attics. Dealers and collectors alike were aware of what was happening to our business. So, by the time I began garage saling in the spring, there weren't as many finds. Phone calls from my ad were dwindling. Prices people demanded for their toy trains were astronomical. Toy trains I found in "junk" condition were priced at hundreds of dollars, when their actual resale value was twenty to fifty dollars. Priced out of the train shows, I had to find other ways to continue in the toy train business.

It was time for a change in my life for other reasons, as well. The stresses and the drudgery of travel, loading and unloading the car, and more, led me to act on my dream of owning a hobby shop. The best ideas of where and how to start came from Tom Riley, a hobby shop owner and friend, who, himself, started in a flea market.

"Ya know, ya might think of getting a booth at Country Fair Flea Market, the way I did. Ya could easily make a few hundred dollars a week there," suggested Tom.

"Yeah, I've been thinking a lot about doing that," I agreed.

"There wouldn't be all that traveling, loading and unloading. And in a flea market, ya'd qualify as a bonafide hobby shop, so ya could sell new stuff as well as used stuff."

The very next morning, Good Friday, I went to the County Building in Mt. Clemens and filed my assumed name: Phil's Place – Trains and Hobbies. I shopped area markets and settled on the one Tom recommended. During the wait for an opening, I built an elaborate booth, my own miniature hobby shop. That July, Dick Serreyn, a friend, helped move the booth into the market on a sticky-hot Friday evening. Despite the lack of air conditioning and late night shoppers climbing over us while we were on our hands and knees setting up, by closing time we had the booth assembled and ready for the Saturday rush Tom promised.

In the sweltering heat that night, I couldn't sleep. I tossed and turned until 1:45 a.m. I knew that a drink of wine would ease the stress and help me sleep. It could also be the end of my dream if it got hold of me again. Still, I dressed and drove to the convenience store for my first jug of wine in two years. I was hysterical knowing that I was throwing away two years of sobriety, but I couldn't handle the stress without it.

When I got home, I went to the kitchen sink and opened the wine. I filled two wine glasses to their brims, then poured the rest of the wine down the drain. Now I had what I needed to get me where I wanted to go. I gulped the two glasses of wine and staggered to bed.

Saturday's heat was in the sweltering 90s. I knew the flea market would be like an oven, meaning I'd have to wear shorts, something I never wanted to do in public, being self-conscious about my body. Still groggy from the wine, and feeling in a shroud of doom, I arrived at the market and made ready for all the business that never came.

By Sunday evening, I had all of five dollars worth of sales for my grand opening weekend. I really couldn't see how I was going to make this venture go. Nevertheless, I ordered stock from the wholesale houses, thinking I'd have something customers could buy. On the second weekend, I arrived early to add my new stock and rearrange my display. By 9:00 p.m. I had no sales, so I closed my booth and headed home dejected. On the way, I bought a jug of wine to drink myself to sleep.

An Awakening

Time dragged on. Each weekend was a clone of the one before it. Through mid-fall, I gave my new venture everything I had, and still no real sales. Christmas was approaching. Sales would surely pick up in November, I thought. I did everything possible to make the business work. I joined the Handicappers Business Association, an organization of business people with disabilities. I returned to A.A., but I could not stay sober. Something had to change soon or I was a dead man for sure.

Desperate to escape my problems and identify with something bigger than myself, I began waking up to Mark Scott, a local "give 'em hell" talk show host. His groupies, who called themselves Tax Protestors, held local meetings, which I began to attend. I very much wanted to fit in the group. I agreed with their philosophy, but I didn't like their tactics.

Then it happened. One sunny Monday morning, no Mark Scott. In his place was a new format. The strange, charismatic voice sounded like a radio preacher. As I sat at my kitchen table drinking my morning coffee, needing someone to share my problems with, I listened to the voice.

"You are what you are. You are who you are, because of what's gone into your head. You can change what you are. You can change who you are by changing what goes into your head."

I never heard these ideas before. But because of the work I did with Steve Campbell, I knew what they meant. The voice only lasted three minutes. Then another voice came in.

"That was the one and only Zig Ziglar."

As a song began, I wondered, "Who in the world is Zig Ziglar?"

After the song, another voice began.

"You got to be hungry! You got to want something bad enough to go out and fight for it. Work day and night for it. In all you dream and scheme about, with the help of God, you are sure to get it."

Who was this guy, I wondered? What was going on here? After another song, the announcer came on.

"This is WBRB, 1430 on your dial. The Motivationnn ... Stationnn!"

I kept listening daily to the morning program. I heard more three- to five-minute excerpts from the great motivational speakers: Zig Ziglar, Les Brown, Mark Victor Hansen, and Jack Boland, pastor of the fastest-growing Unity church in America, The Church Of Today.

SUCCESS?

The Monday before the traditional magical retail selling day after Thanksgiving, I spoke with Tom.

"Have ya got enough R.C. cars for Friday?" Tom asked.

"Just the one I use for display. I don't want to pour more money into the booth," I said.

"If ya don't have the stuff, how do ya expect to make any money?"

"I guess you're right."

"Remember, ya make 80% of ya profit off 20% of ya merchandise. Ya better see ya friend Pat at P&D Wholesale and get about ten more cars," Tom suggested.

I didn't know what to do. Ten more cars would be another $750 I would sink into something that hadn't shown a profit for almost five months now. Every instinct was telling me not to buy any more cars. But I trusted Tom's advice. I bought ten R.C. cars and had them in my booth the day before Thanksgiving. I was ready for the onslaught!

Friday came full tilt with all the hustle and bustle of the day after Thanksgiving. After a big breakfast at Bob Evans, I headed for the market and found myself caught in traffic the whole drive. The market was open early, and stayed open for nine hours: noon 'til nine. The hordes of customers never came. In fact, attendance was below average that entire weekend. The shoppers were at the malls! I wanted this venture to work and had put my entire soul into it, yet on the biggest shopping day of the year, nothing! Feelings of rejection were clouding my mind. I bought a jug of wine. I knew what damage I was doing. My wine had become my lover and my intimate friend once again.

Another Savior

By the third week in December, business had not improved. All of the market dealers were feeling the pinch, but this was no consolation. My back was against a wall with no way to turn. I felt like chucking the whole thing and drinking myself to death. There had to be a way out of this mess, and my spirit would find it.

In mid-December the Handicappers Business Association held a seminar on Growing Your Business. I decided to attend. The speaker was Dr. Raymond Genick. The seminar was in the old Kresge Headquarters, just three blocks from the League for the Handicapped. The building had barriers galore, including a long flight of steps to the front door.

Once in the building, I walked down the dark dingy hallway and entered the room, where a man was writing and drawing on a blackboard. A spark of energy came over me as I took a seat.

"Hi, my name is Phil."

"I'm Ray Genick. Awful weather out there tonight."

"Yeah, that's why I am here early."

I sensed something different about this man, something inspiring. During our brief exchange of greetings, I saw qualities in this man I wanted for myself. Soon other people began to file in, most of whom seemed to know Ray.

As Ray began, he said that businesses are conditioned to fail by the thoughts the owners have about themselves. Then he demonstrated his point. He asked everyone to reproduce his drawing on the blackboard on a piece of paper. The drawing was a box divided into four squares. The first square had an "i" without the dot. The second square had PB, MB and BB written inside. The third square had a rectangle divided into four smaller rectangles side by side. The last square had three words in it: Egg, Rug, and Sex.

First, he asked us to put a dot "ON" the "i." I caught this and put a dot on the shaft of the "i." The next box had a story about Papa Bull, Mama Bull, and Baby Bull. They were in the pasture, when Baby Bull hurt his hoof. Ray said to circle who Baby Bull was most likely to run to, Papa Bull or Mama Bull? Next, Ray said to write the word "Life" in third box, putting one letter in each of the four smaller boxes. Lastly, he said to circle the word in the fourth square that is not compatible with the other two.

"Now," he said, "How many of you put the dot over the "i" like you have been conditioned? I asked you to put the dot "ON" the "i."

Everyone cringed. I did put the dot on the shaft of my "i."

"Next, if you circled Mama Bull, you're wrong, because there is no such creature as a Mama Bull."

All laughed, even me.

"OK. How many printed the word "life" instead of writing it like I asked you to do?"

More laughter and consternation from the participants.

"See we all have been conditioned to print whenever we see a series of boxes. Finally, the word that is not compatible is Sex. Why? Because you can beat an egg and you can beat a rug, but you sure can't beat sex!"

The people laughed and applauded. I sat in awe. For the next two hours, I realized just how much I knew about business. Some of his points were just common sense. Other points were things I did back when I was making pot holders and selling them door to door. Afterward, I told Dr. Genick I would like to talk to him. He told me to call his office and make an appointment for next week.

I wrapped up the Christmas season with $3,000 in sales, ending the year with a $700 profit on the books. The seven hundred certainly didn't reflect the money I had borrowed over the last six months to add stock and pay the rent. And my bank account didn't show that seven hundred. With the pointers Ray gave me in the weeks following the new year, I found ways to make the booth hold its own; though the steady two to three hundred dollars a week I had expected to generate never came.

ANOTHER MENTOR

During the following year, I began to feel better about myself and my goals. While attending the political group, I met Paul Scharfenberg. We talked for a long time one night at the meeting about the flea market and what I was doing. Paul came to the market late the next Sunday afternoon. I was already in the process of closing after another less-than-exciting weekend. We talked for the next hour about how he, too, was interested in the same dream of building this into a great antique and hobby shop. We agreed to work the booth together, seeing where we could take this venture.

The next Friday evening, Paul had arrived ahead of me. Not only was he doing business, but he was cutting up my beautiful booth.

"What are you doing?" I shouted coming up the aisle.

"I'm rearranging, the way we talked about doing last week."

"Yeah, we only talked about doing this. I didn't think we were going to hack it up the first day!"

"Why not? The sooner we change it the sooner we attract more business. We need more light. And we need to keep the people on the *outside*, not opened the way you had it."

I pondered what was going on.

"Aw, hell. You got the damn thing cut up, you might as well go ahead and finish what you're doing," I gave in.

What had come to be known as the most attractive booth in the market was being downgraded to look like all the rest. I accepted the stripped-down version of my booth. At least I had someone to help make the dream of a hobby shop a reality. With Paul helping out in the booth, I decided I had an opportunity to do train shows again. I always knew there was more money to be made there. I put my ad back in the newspaper and the calls began to trickle in.

One day around five in the afternoon, I was napping on the couch when the phone rang. For some strange reason I recognized the voice. It had been five years since I had priced his collection at over $3,000. I had taken Don, my collector friend, along to help negotiate. But instead, Don had talked the man out of the deal. Don was a collector and not a dealer, and I learned the difference in the way they think. Now, five years later, the man was calling again and ready to sell.

This time I called Dick, who drove with me to the house to help me reappraise the collection. Whatever it was, call it "Divine Inspiration," my inner voice never failed to give me the right price to offer for a collection. Obviously, the man wanted more than the eight hundred dollars I bid five years ago. I knew I could start at one thousand. I didn't know exactly why that number, but I figured I could play with another thousand for his three thousand worth of trains. To my surprise the man took the one thousand on the spot. This was the biggest and the most profitable transaction I ever completed.

The next night, Dick and Paul helped me bring the collection to my house. It filled all three of our cars. After Paul and I sorted it, I called another collector friend, Cliff. He was there in 30 minutes. Cliff bought seven hundred dollars worth that night and three hundred the next, returning my initial investment. The following Sunday, at one of the biggest train shows of the year, Paul and I sold another thousand dollars. The third thousand took several trains shows over the next few months to realize.

I thought the combination of the flea market and the train shows would carry Paul and I on to prosperity. I thought Paul and I were on our way. He could keep the booth going in the flea market and I would do the train shows.

Anne

Everything was going the way I thought it should. I began attending a support group other than A.A. that was sponsored by the Cerebral Palsy Center. I had my usual reservations about going, but when I arrived I found that everything about the center was different. In fact, few if any of the people remembered Mrs. Schilling. At first, it seemed like everyone was crying the blues about having Cerebral Palsy. When I started talking about accepting it and making the best with what you have, I felt the coldness in the room. The last thing any of these people wanted to hear was learning to accept their Cerebral Palsy!

That first night I also met the answer to my prayers. Her name was Anne.

After seeing each other at a few meetings, she asked me to give her a call, which I did. From that first date for coffee, we found we had a lot in common. Anne was very talented and could even play Mozart on the piano! A person with Cerebral Palsy playing Mozart?

After the coffee date, I asked Anne to go to the movies. When the house lights went down, the chemistry started. Anne let me put my arm around her. About a half hour into the movie I found her blouse opened. I laid my hand just inside, feeling the warmth of her body. I didn't allow myself to venture further. After the movie we went for coffee and talked for hours.

I wanted Anne to see my independence, so I invited her to my place the day before one of the meetings for a home-cooked supper by candlelight and for a tour of my model railroad. In the back of my mind, I was also hopeful nature would take its course. After the tour of my model railroad, supper was simmering on the stove, Anne and I sat on the sofa and embraced with a passionate kiss. I felt feelings I hadn't felt in years.

"Are you seeing anyone else?" Anne asked in a small seductive tone.

We were staring in each other's eyes.

"Not as of this moment," I returned softly.

As our conversation turned to intimate things, Anne nodded her head. I knew what that meant. I slowly unbuttoned her blouse, pulled it back over her shoulders, and dropped it off her arms. I quickly pulled my shirt off. Anne turned her back to me as I kissed her neck. She slowly unhooked her bra strap and let it fall forward off her body. When she turned toward me, her beauty was breathtaking. I laid my head across her breast and suckled her. I saw a look of love on Anne's face.

As Anne moved her hands to her slacks to pull them off, I said, "No! Stop! What we have here is too precious to be doing this now."

Anne responded with a soft whisper. "OK. Yeah, I think you are right. We can wait."

We dressed, and enjoyed our supper. We talked about the future, exchanging hopes and dreams. I told Anne about what I had learned on the radio about having dreams and goals. After supper and the dishes, followed by a few long romantic hugs on the sofa, we left for the support group meeting.

During the two-hour meeting, it was apparent to me that Anne was in love with me. I heard more excitement in her voice than anytime before. Again, during the drive home, we continued our discussion of our future and our feelings for one another. In her driveway, I stopped the car and scooted close to her for a last hug and a kiss. As I opened her coat for my hug, I couldn't help but see that her blouse was open and, sometime before we had left the meeting, she had removed her bra.

I wanted to spread her coat and blouse off her shoulders, but I stopped. I pulled her coat closed, then hugged her warmly and planted a passionate kiss on her lips.

"Anne, if this relationship is going to be as good as I feel it will be, we can wait for this."

Again, in her tender tone of voice, Anne replied, "Yeah."

We got out of the car and walked to her door. Half way to the house, the front door inevitably opened and there stood her Mama. My excitement vanished with her appearance, but during the drive home that night, I knew Anne was the one for me.

As our relationship intensified over the next few weeks, we visited my mother. Anne and Mama were a hit. They were drawn to each other, and the evening proved a success. However, the negative voice inside kept saying, "No, she's not the one. This is not right." I chose to ignore it and focused on the positive.

ZIG ZIGLAR

In the meantime, I kept my garage saling going with Paul's help at the flea market. With the profits from the huge train collection and Anne in my life, I felt I was on my way to achieving my dreams. The radio was motivating me from morning to night. One time, the disc jockey announced the appearance of Zig Ziglar. I didn't hear all of the details, so when I returned home in the afternoon, I called the station for the 800 number for more information. Then I called to reserve two seats for me and Anne.

"I'm very sorry, we're sold out. But he'll be back in the area in November," I was told by the woman on the other end of the line. I was shocked that the tickets were forty dollars apiece. All the money I made on the big collection was put toward the debt incurred by the flea market. I really had no disposable income.

"Well, er ... see we have Cerebral Palsy," I said. " And..."

"Then, we could give you a scholarship for the seminar," she offered.

"That's great!" I said.

"The seminar starts at seven. Get there at 6:30, and we can help you get into the hotel."

"No. That won't be necessary. We are capable of getting in and out of any place we choose to go."

After we finished making other arrangements, I thanked the woman, who said the tickets would arrive within the week. When the tickets came, I was excited that I was finally going to see and hear the voice that captivated me all these weeks on the radio.

Anne, No!

Nine o'clock the next morning the phone rang. It was Anne.

"I don't want to ever see you again!"

"What!" I exclaimed. "What in the hell is happening? The last time I saw you, we were madly in love."

"My mother came into my room this morning demanding to know if I was going to marry you."

"Marry you? Hell, we don't even know each other yet! Let's not talk of marriage until we know who each other really is." Click the phone was dead.

I overcame the pain that was trying to grip my being and turned to my tried and true remedy, flowers. Flowers were a sign of tenderness and love. I sent Anne a bouquet of roses. I had no way of preventing her from hanging up on me again, but I prayed for the phone to ring. In about an hour the phone rang. It was Anne again, in tears.

"Did you call the police?" Anne asked between her sobs.

"Why would I call the police?" I answered, confused.

"Someone called the police and told them I was trying to kill myself!" she said.

I sat in my chair in shock. What in the hell is going on? The relationship was over. I knew it. I told Anne about the roses that would be coming that afternoon. But she said nothing that told me what she was thinking. It was no use. Anne, and perhaps her mother, were caught up in some lousy way of thinking and I couldn't do anything to change it. I hadn't learned from any of my prior relationships, it seemed, and instead, had fallen into the same trap once again. Predictably, to relieve my pain, I made the trip to the drugstore for a jug of wine.

Motivational Speaker!

The following Tuesday, it was unusually warm and foggy for the middle of November. I spent the day anticipating Zig Ziglar's talk, and headed out into the fog with plenty of time to spare, avoiding the rush hour traffic by taking every other shortcut I knew for the forty-mile trek to the hotel. My plan didn't work. There was construction and subsequent traffic tie-ups along every route. I felt God was testing my patience. Arriving almost on time, I found the hotel and parked. To my horror, there was a revolving door. Bad enough. But this door was continuously revolving. I couldn't believe what I was seeing. I tried the side doors, but to make it more challenging for me, the side doors were locked. I had to make it through the revolving door, or not at all. Timing myself I made it in and through without incident.

When I found the room where Zig Zigler was to speak, the people at the reception table were expecting me. They escorted me into the room to a seat in the second row. For some reason, I didn't want to be in the first row. Sitting there by myself, I looked around at the many chairs that had been set up. I estimated there were about five thousand chairs set up. At forty dollars apiece, someone was making a killing. My aloneness in all this space began to trigger old feelings of insecurity. I began to wonder what I was doing there. Then, I thought about Anne and how this time I had hoped that everything was going to work. Christmas was coming. I thought about ideas for a surprise gift to reestablish communication between us.

Within a half hour, the crowd started filtering in. The room filled fast. Finally, Zig came out and mingled with the people. He is the only speaker who does this. Many come out and give their speech and, in a flash, they're gone. Not Zig Ziglar. As Zig started his presentation, I hung on to every word. "You are what you are...you are who you are...because of what's gone into your head. You can change what you are...you can change who you are...by changing what goes into your head!" I was mesmerized the whole first hour. It was during the second hour, just before the middle break, I began to let my mind wander. My life flashed through my consciousness. I thought, "If there is anyone who has a challenging life, it's me. Do I have a story to tell!"

At the break, I decided to buy the book Zig was pushing, *See You At The Top*. For the first time in my life, I didn't allow the crowd to deter me from going to the table where the books and tapes were being sold. I made my way to the table, picked up the book and pulled a twenty from my billfold. The girl at the table motioned me to put the twenty back in my pocket. I returned to the room and got into the autograph line so Zig could autograph my book. He wrote: "Phil, Zig Ziglar, Eph. 2: 8&9. I knew those passages. They were the two passages upon which Martin Luther built his doctrine. I sat down again and pondered the message I had just received. I felt strange. I felt a presence I had never known before. I returned home mightily motivated.

DEPRESSION AGAIN!

That's when what should have been my greatest Thanksgiving ever turned out to be the beginning of another deep depression. This was the disastrous weekend at the flea market, which was followed by a series of dismal weekends through the holidays. I drank heavily. I forgot I had a story to tell. I felt my life was finished. I wanted out.

For some reason, I continued going to the support group and A.A. Something deep down inside felt there was something I needed to accomplish in this life. Back in A.A., I felt cheated since none of these people had to live the hell I was living. There were many nights I'd buy a jug of wine on the way home from the meetings. After I was drunk, I would call Mama and blame her for all of my problems. That Christmas, too, is one I would rather forget. Sales were seventy percent below the year before. Even Paul turned out to be a big disappointment. Maybe God was telling me to never again become dependent on others.

One day in mid-December, I got out of bed not knowing what to do. I turned the radio on and the first speaker out of the chute again was Zig Ziglar. The voice motivated me once again as it always did. That afternoon I picked up Zig's book and started to read it. I was never much of a reader, but the book mesmerized me. I read all morning. I read the entire book in less than two weeks — a record for me.

More importantly, after reading the book, I started putting some of the practices to work. One in particular was to slap my hands together in the morning and say, "It's a great day to get up and go get 'em!" I felt stupid doing it, but what the hell, it sure can't get any worse, I thought.

Then, I wanted another book to read. Since Maxwell Maltz was one of the voices on the radio, I decided to read his book, *Psycho-Cybernetics*. It was all the rage some ten rears earlier, when I joined A.A. Unfortunately, my current sponsor told me not to read the book, since it wasn't on the A.A. list. Like a good little boy, I did what he said. In fact, I threw the book out.

FINDING THE CHURCH

January was not one of my favorite months of the year. But this January, I began to understand how I got to where I was in life. Thinking every morning as I listened to the motivational speakers on the radio, I visualized my life over the years and thought of all of the life lessons I had learned the hard way. Again the thought of becoming a motivational speaker crossed my mind. It seemed like a crazy thought. "Me! A motivational speaker?" Then I remembered Zig said to write a goal on a piece of paper. As depressed as I was, and although I was drinking again before going to bed, I thought, "Oh, hell, I haven't got a damn thing to lose." I took a yellow note pad and a black marker and wrote: I AM A MOTIVATIONAL SPEAKER FOR PEOPLE WITH HANDICAPS. I taped it on my kitchen wall, then toasted it with another glass of wine.

By the second week in January, things were beginning to improve. Mama was doing some of my housework, though I hated having her do it. It made me feel like I was still her poor little boy. One day as she cleaned, I wanted her to listen to the speakers on the radio, which had become my lifeline, the link to my future. Mama thought it was just another of my many obsessions. She told me so. Then, during the day's programming, I noticed something different. It seemed that all the people at the station were sad about something. Mama had left for the day and I was about to have supper when it happened. At 5 p.m. the entire staff went on the air and said together, "This has been The Motivation Station. WBRB. 1430. Goodbye." Then static! The one thing keeping me going was WBRB. Now it was gone!

The next morning I slept until noon. When I turned the radio on to FM, all it played were sad love songs. Sitting at my kitchen table drinking coffee, I looked at the piece of paper hanging on the wall. I thought, "Well, Zig, if you are right, here's to it!" I knew I had to do something to keep the voices of motivation in my life. I dressed and went to a bookstore and bought a Zig Ziglar motivational tape. I didn't even own a cassette player, but Paul Scharfenberg gave me an old tape player of his to use.

I returned to therapy at the mental health center. Working with Charlotte Arkins, she helped me cope with the loss of Anne, as well as the radio station.

One evening, after another trying day, I read in the newspaper that Og Mandino, another speaker I had heard on the radio was going to be speaking at The Church Of Today, Jack Boland's Unity church. Jack was well-known throughout the A.A. community. Many of the people I associated with called Jack a con artist. But I had listened to him on the radio Sunday mornings driving to the train shows. I had called his telephone messages every night, while I was going through my divorce.

I remembered the night, five years before, when I drove to the church to hear one of the radio talk show hosts from WBRB. I went inside and took one look at the crowd and ran out. I drove off so fast, I almost hit a car at the corner. "Well," I thought, "that was five years ago. If this church is a place where I can see motivational speakers, I'll give them a call." When I found out there was a speaker every Wednesday, I made up my mind to go.

The following Wednesday, as frightened as I was, I walked in the door and was greeted by a man named Andy. I felt something special about Andy as he took me into the sanctuary. When I saw the broadcast video cameras set up, I knew something special was going on here. Later, as first-time visitors were asked to stand up, I stood up! I surprised myself! I had never done anything like that before, because I was always too embarrassed to call attention to myself.

Then, the lesson began. The speaker was Michael Murphy, an associate minister, who sounded a lot like the voice of Jack Boland. By the end of the lesson, I had had enough. These people were too good for me. I wanted out of the place, NOW!

On my beeline out of the church, something caught my eye and stopped me dead in my tracks. Through the glass in the church office, I spotted on a cabinet a Lionel Engine, a GP9. What is a Lionel GP9 engine doing in a church office? Whatever the positive spiritual energy was, I felt it from Andy, plus my fascination with the video cameras and the mystery of the train engine there were enough to keep me coming back each Wednesday.

After a few weeks, I was looking forward to Wednesday afternoons, especially the greeting I got from Andy. "Fabulous Phil," Andy called me. More importantly, the Wednesday lessons were making sense. More and more, thoughts about my life, where I came from and where Jack Boland and his associates told me I could be going were beginning to make a impression on my consciousness. Although there were days I swore I would never set foot in that so-called church again, by the following Wednesday I was back there making sure everyone saw me in that first row on the right of the speaker.

By the end of March, the lessons were having an effect. I had several pieces of paper on my kitchen wall with affirmations on them. I had stayed sober for two months, when I hadn't been able to do that for nine years on my own. And I had begun to try some of the support groups that met at the church that Jack Boland had pushed from the pulpit like a side show barker. I went to the Monday evening A.A. group, which was a unique experience. The people were more friendly than any other A.A. group I had ever attended. What really impressed me was that the members seemed to be changing their lives. I didn't hear the same old "Ain't Life Awful" I heard and felt so many times. Most affirming for me, I was coming to believe I could change my life. I felt that these people all seemed to know what it took and were willing to do the work to make things happen.

fantastic idea

With spring in the air, I was able to pick up with my garage saling, to kill time more than anything else. What was really nibbling away at the back of my mind was the thought of becoming a motivational speaker. I scheduled another meeting with Ray Genick to discuss the idea with him.

"Ray, I've an idea that is kinda off the wall. I think I want to be a motivational speaker," I said with some hesitation, expecting a negative reaction.

Instead, Ray jumped right in with, "I think that's a fantastic idea, Phil! When do you want to start?" Ray went on. "I have a business administration class next week. You should talk to them about all the businesses you have started."

I was stunned! I didn't know what to do or say, next. I had come in expecting a discussion. Now, I had my first speaking engagement in ten days! I could only commit to the date, feeling I had to put my money where my mouth was. We visited for a while longer. Then I headed home without a clue as to what I would present to Ray's class.

I made myself a cup of coffee when I arrived home. As I sat at the kitchen table, facing me on the wall was my goal sheet: "I am a motivational speaker for people with handicaps."

"OK," I thought. "I wanted this. Now, I have to do this." I began jotting ideas on a pad. Soon I began to see a speech taking shape. I knew from several A.A. talks I had given that once I got going, more ideas would come to mind. More than an A.A. open talk, however, this was the beginning of something big that started with an idea on a piece of paper that I hung on the wall when I was drunk!

THE SPEECH

On Thursday, I packed a portable tape recorder and my handwritten notes and headed for Ray's offices. Ray and about twelve students were seated around a horseshoe table arrangement when I walked in. I took a seat in the corner and waited for Ray's cue. Ray introduced me as a entrepreneur who was going to explain how to build self-esteem and work toward a goal. I certainly didn't feel I was the guy Ray was introducing, but soon it was me up at the podium.

I started badly. First, I fumbled with the recorder, and I couldn't read my handwritten notes. I began to shuffle them, trying to make sense of the flow. The voice of my fourth grade teacher echoed in my mind like the rumble of distant thunder, "You can't do this!" Something inside stood its ground and had control. The fear passed as quickly as it came. With a deep breath, I opened my mouth and the words flowed smoothly. I made eye contact and saw Ray's students hanging onto my every word. Some were taking notes. I saw Ray, himself, marvel as I described my many attempts to make an independent living for myself. Forty-five minutes passed. With a closing charge of "Excelsior!" I accepted applause and took a barrage of questions for another fifteen or twenty minutes. Soaked with perspiration, I was tired and wanted to get home, but I stayed until class ended, and received a thank you and a handshake from Ray.

Later that afternoon, after a nap, I played the tape. As I listened, I was aware that I was hearing someone I did not know. No high-pitched panic in this voice. No anger. No frustration. No swallowed vowels. No slurred consonants. Rather, there was a command of language and a level of confidence I seldom felt on a day-to-day basis. This was another me. This was a motivated me.

I flashed back to what I told Les Brown, the professional motivator, two weeks prior, when I attended his talk at my old church. "Hi, I'm Philip Schmucker. I am going to be a motivational speaker." I remembered how Les had gestured politely and shaken hands, discounting my goal. I remembered meeting up with Les again in the church basement with my partner Paul, and how Les invited Paul to bring "your friend Phil to my office." I had to jump in at that point to tell Les that I had brought Paul, not the other way around.

"You don't understand, Les. I am my own boss."

It was then that Les set a noon appointment for me to visit him in his offices in downtown Detroit the following Monday. That was the Monday before my speech at Ray Genick's class. Les stood me up that Monday and again that Friday, even after he rescheduled. I had little more to say to Les Brown than the simple message I left with his service.

"You tell Les Brown he missed seeing the greatest handicapped motivational speaker in the world!"

After another false start at connecting, Les called to apologize for personal complications that had affected his business schedule. We talked a long time. Then, he invited me to his next seminar in a backhanded way.

"Are you going to be here Saturday?"

"Be where?" I asked.

"At my seminar. I am inviting you to learn how to speak."

"I'll be there," I responded without hesitation.

The Saturday seminar was in a conference room in Les' office building. The room contained about eight round tables on which were packets of materials for each seminar participant. As the seminar started, information was flowing from Les faster than the participants could absorb it. I was dazzled by the abundance of information he presented. The agenda included brief speeches by each participant from our places.

During the lunch break, another participant came up to me just as I was about to dig into my salad.

"Hi, I'm Gary LaLonde. I've been watching you all morning. You sure don't seem to let your Cerebral Palsy get in your way."

"No. If I did, my life wouldn't be worth living. It's taken hard work in psychotherapy to get where I am today."

"Have you ever tried hypnotherapy?" Gary asked, as he pulled his business card from his breast pocket.

"No," I said, looking at his card. "But that doesn't mean I might not give it a try."

"Well, it's not as spooky as people make it out to be," he smiled.

"Fine. I'll give you a call," as he handed me a cassette tape, then returned to his table.

The afternoon session pushed me way beyond my physical and emotional tolerance levels. Increasingly edgy, I wanted to go home, but, at the same time, I didn't want to miss anything. Everyone, including both Les and Gary, saw how disruptive I can become.

On the drive home, that negative voice inside said the thing for me to do was to buy a jug of wine, enjoy a couple drinks, and forget this foolish dream. The other, more constructive inner voice suggested that I not stop, but get home first. "Just get home," it suggested. "If you still want a drink, you can always run out to the store later." I pressed on and passed by the party store.

When I walked in the door and checked my answering machine for messages, the light was blinking. It was a message from Gary LaLonde. It was one of the most encouraging and inspiring messages I had ever received. He reminded me to play the tape he had given to me. I immediately played the tape. The story was about Roger Crawford, a man born with withered limbs, who became a motivational speaker. His story motivated me to follow my dream. It also saved me from drinking myself into a stupor that night. The following week, Gary and I started several months of hypnosis therapy, which produced subtle positive changes in my thinking.

Telling My Story On Cassette

As the summer progressed, I closed the booth in the flea market. I had a feeling I was destined for bigger and better things. I spent more and more time at the Church Of Today, attending services, seminars, and taking part in other activities. I joined Toastmasters. I marveled from behind the lectern how my enunciation became clear and my thoughts flowed.

There was magic in my public speaking voice that no one could hear at any other time.

Motivated by the tape Gary LaLonde gave me, and knowing I had a powerful story about myself to tell, I decided to produce an audio tape to sell. To write and record a thirty-minute audiotape was going to really take some effort. Using what I learned from Les Brown and Ray Genick, plus what I knew from experience, I banged out a script I called, "Dreams, Perseverance, and Choices." It was the best I thought I could do. With Ray's help, I found someone to record and edit, but I did everything else, using what I learned from the Les Brown seminar. I even wrote and designed the "J" card insert for the cassette box. I was ready to start my speaking career and conquer the world.

Dream Come True

During the work on my audiotape, I met Detroit TV personality Jerry Stanecki at the Church Of Today. He had come by the church to attend a seminar I also happened to be attending one evening. I had viewed his series of personal profiles of "Extraordinary People," so I introduced myself.

"Jerry, my name is Philip Schmucker. I'm going to be a motivational speaker."

In his deep, velvety voice, Jerry said, "Give me your name and number."

I didn't have a business card. In fact, I didn't even carry paper and a pen at the time. Using his pen and the back of one of his cards, I wrote my name and number.

"Can you read it?"

"Sure."

During the seminar that night, we all took turns sharing at our table. Jerry spoke third. Later, I spoke. Immediately after I finished, Jerry left the table and the room. I thought he'd be right back, but he didn't return to the group that night or ever.

Six months later, while I continued to develop my audiotape script, the phone rang early one Monday morning.

"Phil, this is Jerry (Stanecki). I'll be out there tomorrow to interview you."

"OK," I said, still half asleep and not realizing what he was really saying. "Who is...?" I began to ask as my head cleared.

"Jerry Stanecki."

"Oh, yeah, Jerry. Yeah, sure. Tomorrow will be fine."

"Ten a.m."

"OK."

After I hung up the phone, the reality sunk in. I looked around at my surroundings and realized, "Oh, God, I can't let Jerry see this place the way it is." When it came to housework, I always came up short. I spent the rest of the day cleaning the town house. As excited as I was about the interview, I felt I wasn't worthy. Something in me was still denying my value and worth as a person.

The next morning, Tuesday, my alarm clock did not ring! I woke at 9:30 by my wrist watch. The alarm clock read 9:00. I went downstairs to turn on the radio. Nothing. The power was off! "Oh, God, no." I couldn't shave ... no lights ... no power ... what are we going to do!?"

When Jerry pulled up promptly at ten with his small TV crew, I met them on my front porch in a panic. I explained that the power was off. Then, as if by magic, it came back on. After a quick tour of the house, I could tell he was amazed with what he saw, especially my model railroad, complete with the scenery and mountains running along the basement walls. He was at a loss for words.

We began the interview while I shaved. Jerry repeated his questions in several "takes" to be sure he had a variety of shots with audio that could be cut to make the story. I understood the process and cooperated fully. Jerry remarked how I seemed to instinctively know what was going on in the process and how I was coming off like I had been doing interviews all my life. After the direct interview was completed, the crew taped "B-roll" shots for cutaways, like close-ups of the railroad. As Jerry was leaving, I heard him say to the cameraman, "This is too big for three minutes. This should be a full hour on PBS!"

Two weeks later, the interview was aired. It got mixed reviews from

Mama and the rest of the family, probably because I told the world for the first time just who Daddy was. The only person who seemed to agree with my description of Daddy was Emmett.

Three weeks after the interview aired, Jerry called back and we talked for a long time. I sent Jerry a copy of my finished audiotape for his feedback. He later called to tell me it was a piece of garbage. In my heart I knew he was right. I knew I could and would do better. Jerry coached me through a rewrite of the audiotape script. It was during this difficult process that the idea of writing a book came to mind again. But how could I begin a book when I could hardly put together a script for a thirty-minute audiotape? How could I physically write a 200-page book manuscript? All I had to work with was my old IBM electric typewriter. Besides, I couldn't spell worth a damn.

Ray and I discussed these issues during one of my visits.

"I can teach you how to use a word processor right here," Ray said.

As simply as that, I began word processing classes, during which I learned how computers work. The spellchecker feature alone unlocked my potential, allowing me to truly open up and easily express myself without worry about misspelled words or accidental typos. I could use my complete vocabulary, adding new words along the way, and as long as I could phonetically come close, the computer did its damnest to spell it right. A quick read-through caught words that sounded alike, but were spelled differently, like "then" and "than."

Jerry also helped motivate me to improve my writing by taking some inspiration from movies. I hadn't seen a movie since my last movie date. One Saturday, he called to simply get me out of the house, and suggested I see a certain film. It paid off. When I got home after the show, I sat right down and composed:

> "Looking across the meadow, I could see the lush green grass. The light breeze was licking my cheeks with the gentleness of a lover. The tall green grass was being blown to and fro. I heard the melody of the wind as it howled about my being."

When I looked at what I had written, I felt goose bumps. I called Jerry immediately and read the sentences to him.

"Man, that's quite a paragraph! Where did it come from?" he asked.

"I just saw it and heard it and felt it," I said. "It happened after I went to the movie."

"The movie did that to you? I think you better start going to at least three movies a week."

"Yeah!" I agreed.

I actually went back to the theather that night and saw *Field Of Dreams*, about a man who hears a voice that inspires him to turn a cornfield into a baseball stadium. "If you build it, he will come," a voice promises. Watching the movie, I felt God's presence in my own life. On the way home, I heard a similar voice telling me, "Write the book and they will read it." A movie fantasy, no doubt. However, the voice did not fade away with the smell of the theater popcorn.

I went back to the typewriter and started typing essays. I worked on them during Ray's computer classes, where I retyped them and cleaned up the spelling. The creative and mechanical freedoms of being able to type any word I chose was actually thrilling. I was soon composing essays at a rate of six hundred words an hour.

The Miracle Continues

While my relationship with Jerry Stanecki strengthened, I began to help him produce a cable TV show. Sitting in the control room, I observed everything that was happening and learned about TV production. At this same time, I had wanted to join the Media Department at the Church Of Today. Bob and Greg the TV directors saw the changes in me and decided to give me a chance.

"Phil, we have watched you grow over the pass few months. The anger we saw in you when you first walked through the doors isn't as strong. Greg and I have decided to let you come aboard the crew," Bob said.

I was overwhelmed. Becoming a member of the media team was the most technical and artistic challenge I had ever been given. Over the next few months I even amazed myself. My so-called "spastic movements" became less pronounced. Greg also became my A.A. sponsor, spending time with me in long, in-depth discussions, which dramatically helped me to focus on my goals.

My ultimate goal to become a motivational speaker kept having ups and downs. I knew it wasn't going to be easy. What I really needed was a book to get me known. I remembered the excerpts of *My Left Foot,* which Mama read to me in the newspaper when I was 10 years old. Steve Campbell's suggestion years before, that I write a book, also came to mind. I thought, perhaps, with my new-found creative freedom to write with a word processor, the time had come to begin the book.

Step one was buying a computer. I settled on an IBM, still terrified I could strike the wrong key and…bang!…everything is erased, the spellchecker locks up, or the drive crashes. I had heard a lot of horror stories about these temperamental machines. Tragedies do happen. However, I am both an expert at imagining them happening, as well as an expert at making them happen. Many times my computer was in danger of its own life. However, Gary LaLonde and others successfully helped me channel my frustrations and stresses into creative writing.

How to begin writing my life story was a puzzle. I stared at the blank screen. Finally, I began by writing memories of people and incidents, weaving them together in a see-saw chronology. I wrote in the third person so I could make editorial comments and point out insights I was having to the reader. It soon became clear that writing in the third person was an easy way to avoid reliving the pain of my life through actual dialogue and first-person narrative. If anyone would have told me the pain of reliving my heartbreaks again, or the time it would take, I would never have begun.

In the beginning, I wrote occasionally, sending my little biographical essays to different "Handicap" newspapers in the area. They were being picked up for publication, but I received mostly negative feedback from the editors and readers. My message was powerful. However, the typical disabled person couldn't accept that we handicapped persons, like all human beings, create most of our own frustration and anger.

Working from some of my essays, I finally sat down one day and created the opening of Chapter 1. I wanted to give myself a beginning, a place in time through the eyes of my Daddy, the dreamer. From the start of Chapter 1, I watched my anger transform into pictures and dialogue…

"It was one of those early April-in-Michigan days, when the southwest breeze is warm, like a lover's caress. A man in his early twenties paced across the plot of land, where he was about to construct his dream castle for his bride…"

Is It Real?

During January, I attended a seminar at a hotel conducted by one of my favorite speakers, Mark V. Hansen. As I sat on a couch in the hotel lobby waiting for my friend Gary, I watched all the people file into the seminar. Among them was the most beautiful woman I had ever seen. This blonde had walked in off a flight from Hollywood! I know we made eye contact as she passed.

"You look like you've seen a vision," Gary said approaching me.

"Yeah!" I said. "Another beautiful woman who I can never meet," I mumbled.

"Man, how many times have I suggested no negative talk?"

Once inside the huge ballroom, over the heads of the audience I immediately spotted the woman. She had an infectious laugh that I was magnetized to. After the seminar, as I was standing in line to greet Mark, I watched her parade around the room. After making eye contact with me one more time, she disappeared.

At the Church Of Today a few weeks later during a morning service, I was running the lights. A little sleepy after getting up at 5 a.m., I was wide awake when I heard that laugh. She was here, in my church! Over the next several Sundays, she returned. I watched her from a distance in the coffee room after every service, followed by a string of eligible men fawning over her. "Out of my league," I thought to myself. Besides, I was having some success rebuilding my relationship with Joyce. It had never been better.

A few weeks later, at the first of the two Sunday services, our minister, Jack Boland, announced he was dying, and proceeded to conduct his own funeral service! He did the same thing at the second service. We were a close community. As controversial and as influential as Jack was in Detroit, his unorthodox means of announcing his news came as a blow to everyone. Still in shock from the first service, and now doubly stunned after the second, I was sitting in the director's chair across from the sound booth when Gerry Verellen, another staff member, brought someone into the control room for a tour. It was her! I was dazzled by the depth of her blue eyes. When our eyes met once again, she smiled and my heart pounded.

The fantasy of this gorgeous woman in my life filtered through my mind during my drive home. She could never be part of my life in reality, of course, but I could dream! Gerry later told me her name was Sally.

Again, after a few weeks passed, I was at the church for a Monday evening Toastmaster meeting. Since I was the Toastmaster for the evening, I arrived early. In walked Sally. She came right up to the first row and sat next to me. I was nervous enough about being Toastmaster, now I stared straight ahead, not wanting her to see how I was affected by her presence. During the meeting, of course, I had to make eye contact. It had to be obvious to everyone, including her, how my eyes were drawn to her. I felt her eyes were drawn to me, as well. Surprising myself at the end of the meeting, I asked Sally to go for coffee, and she accepted!

I had never taken someone to a restaurant who didn't have a disability. We talked for an hour and half, during which I told her how I was attracted to her and asked her how she felt. She simply nodded affirmatively and smiled. Her eyes confirmed my wishes, although I knew this was still my impossible dream. We left the restaurant saying we'd get to know each other better. I kept telling myself on the way home that I was out of my league.

Strange Encounter

As spring turned into summer, the church recovered from the death of Jack. Attendance was on the rise thanks to the efforts of our new minister, Michael Murphy. Each Sunday, I personally greeted Sally in the fellowship hall. It was the one moment each week I looked forward to seeing her. I kept reminding myself who I was and that God had given me Joyce to love.

During this time, Ray Genick and I began to plan my first seminar. Ray had a friend, Jan, who rep'd Nightengale-Conant, to handle the promotion.

At a meeting with Ray and I, Jan said, "Phil, I am going to ask Sally to help out with the seminar." That was fine with me, although I wondered what the connection was between them. I never did learn what Sally's specific seminar duties were.

In the meantime, I read a flier promoting a Sexual Abuse seminar with fine print that read: "A Jan Foster Production." I thought it would be wise to see what kind of presentation she produced. When I pulled into the hotel lot, I parked next to a blue four-door Buick. Not only was it exactly the same color as my VW, the licence plates had the same digits. I also couldn't help noticing the bumper sticker on the trunk lid. It read: INCEST SURVIVOR. Remembering the seminar was on sexual abuse, I thought, "Man this person has been through a living hell!"

Inside, as I scouted the meeting room, I found it rather drab and poorly lit, not a very uplifting, motivational environment. I watched Jan do her thing from a seat midway from the front row. I was looking down at the flyer when I heard Sally's infectious laugh. I looked up and spotted her about three rows in front of me.

Jan's introduction of the speaker, former Miss America, Marilyn Van Derber Atler, was a lot less than I had expected of Jan. The hollow-sounding PA system made it worse. As I lost interest due to the anger the speaker expressed, I increasingly focused on Sally and how she related to the message.

After the seminar, Sally and I exchanged greetings. This was all I allowed myself to do because of the feelings I didn't want to face. Walking back to my car, I pondered the events of the evening, especially about how Jan would handle my seminar. I passed the Buick again noticing the similarities.

My Turn

I didn't see how I was going to be a great speaker. Even though Jan is credited with "making" Michael Wickett his name, according to Ray, I didn't see how she would help me. What I held on to was my role as a valued member of the Church Of Today's Media Department and my weekly exchange of greetings with Sally. Talking to her in the fellowship hall was like looking into the sun. Her smile beamed. Her blue eyes captivated me. When I discovered that the mysterious blue Buick was hers, I thought, "God! Is this a sign?" Immediately the confident inner voice I had learned to pay more attention to answered, "Yes."

One Sunday after church, as Sally and I exchanged greetings, she mentioned Jan had asked her to help with my seminar. I was pleasantly surprised to hear that Jan had followed through. I told Sally I would be grateful for her help, while deep in my soul I knew I didn't want to ever experience the pain of loss I felt when Anne left, or after Joyce and I divorced. I decided then and there to back off from this situation.

Even as planning proceeded for my seminar, I kept plugging away at the book. Everything seemed to be coming along. One August evening, as I was leaving my townhouse for my weekly A.A. meeting, a huge Monarch or Painted Lady butterfly landed on my leg. I couldn't shake it loose! When I did carefully remove it, it didn't take off, it just sat on my porch. I retrieved my Daddy's folding carpenter's rule and measured the wing span at eight inches. Its body was a quarter inch around and six inches long. I had never seen such a large butterfly.

I went next door to my neighbor Augie for a Mason jar. Augie and another neighbor, Ray, came out to see it. I added some milk in the bottom of the jar, then left for my meeting. When I returned, the creature was trying to climb out of the jar. I opened the jar to let it go. When it flew out, it landed on my leg again. What was this thing? A messenger from God? I urged it to take off, and it landed on my shoe. After sitting on my shoe for some time, it suddenly took off up over the roof of my townhouse, never to return. This beautiful thing wanted to be free, but it had almost lost its freedom and its life by visiting me. I have the belief that it would have accepted that fate if it had made me happy to keep it in the jar.

When my big seminar night arrived, I got to the hotel early. The room looked so small! Only fifty chairs had been set up. When Jan arrived alone, without Sally, I didn't ask questions. She appeared to be unorganized. We prayed and then went about our business. I was anxious until Greg arrived with the video gear. Finally, everything began to fall into place. After Jan had drawn my diagram on the chalk board, we were finally ready.

Just before we began, Sally arrived and took a front row seat next to my neighbor, Margaret Spicer. Twelve people were in the audience, including the two top men from the Cerebral Palsy Association, Elmer Cerano and Bill Axtell.

Jan's introduction was rather flat. There was no enthusiasm in her voice. Not what I would expect from a Carnegie graduate. As I began to talk, I could see Sally hanging on to every word. She punctuated every joke with her infectious laugh. After the fastest thirty minutes of my life, my speech was over. There was a standing ovation. I was too tired to see or appreciate any expressions on their faces.

The Invitation

After my presentation, Jan, Sally, another friend Chris, and I went for coffee. When the subject of my book came up, Sally turned the conversation to the book *she* was writing. She knew I was working on a computer, and had borrowed a computer for her writing. She couldn't make it work. Before I knew what I was doing, I offered to see if I could figure it out. She invited me to come to her apartment Saturday morning.

This was the invitation I wanted. But, at the same time, it frightened me. She then mentioned that a new Dale Carnegie course was starting the following week. When I said I had no money to pay for it, she dropped the subject. Driving home that night, I was in a trance. After the euphoria of the presentation and her invitation to her apartment, I was in a state of bliss.

Saturday, as arranged, I arrived promptly at 10 a.m. There was no button at the rear door to call her, so I had to walk what seemed a mile around to the front entrance in order to announce myself. Sally let me in with a bright smile. As I walked into her apartment, I noticed a huge doll house sitting on a piano bench, and on the opposite wall, a doll collection.

The sight of her dolls, many dressed in international costumes, reminded me of Disney's Small, Small World.

Wanting to do just what I agreed to do, I went right to the computer. After half an hour, I couldn't make the computer work. I decided not to frustrate myself any more and said I should probably leave.

"Would you like a cup of coffee?" Sally asked.

I should have said no, but a part of me welcomed the chance. As we talked, subjects I would only discuss with an intimate friend were opened. And, again, she raised the Dale Carnegie class issue.

"Phil, you really should come to Carnegie next week."

"I told you, I can't pay the fee, Sally."

"Don't worry about paying, it'll be taken care of."

She got out her Master Mind Journals and we Master Minded for the money. Master Minding is a form of prayer taught at the church. Two hours had passed. I couldn't stay another minute. Denying my love, I left, feeling I should never see her again.

The following Thursday morning about 10 a.m., the phone rang. It was Sally regarding the Dale Carnegie class that evening. After I again explained my circumstance, I called Diane, the Carnegie instructor.

"Hi, Diane. This is Philip Schmucker. Sally Charles has been insisting that I come to the class tonight. Could you explain to Sally that I can't come to the class. because I can't afford it."

"Sure. I'll tell her you'll take the course when you can pay for it."

About twenty minutes later, the phone rang. It was Diane.

"Phil, I have some great news!"

"Yeah?"

"You can come to class tonight. It has just been paid for."

"By whom?" I asked.

"All I can tell you is that Sally will be your Graduate Assistant."

Each Carnegie Course is a large group divided into smaller working groups. Each small group has a G.A., or Graduate Assistant. Sally's friend, Jan, was also a G.A.

That night, I couldn't focus. My mind kept trying to guess who had paid my tuition. As the twelve gruelling weeks passed, I worked hard and accomplished much. Many nights I wanted to run and never come back, but I made it. It was graduation time. I took Joyce to the ceremony. Sally sat in the back of the room with Jan and the other G.A.s. Each graduate made a final two-minute speech. When it was my turn, Joyce noticed Sally moving closer to the front of the room. I, too, noticed, but discounted it later with Joyce as I drove her home.

"Phil, that woman there, Sally. She's got a yen for you, I can see."

"No," I said. "What would a beautiful woman like her want with me? She can have any man in the church!" I protested.

"Aw, Phil. I know what I saw in her eyes tonight. When you spoke, her face was as bright and radiant as the sun itself!"

Every ounce of my being was trying to deny my true feelings for Sally. Now I was denying it to my ex-wife! Why couldn't I say to the world, "I am in love with Sally Charles!" Why? Because I was clinging to my past and my self-image of an unlovable handicapped man. Sally's greatest gift at this time was being a living incentive to press on. Through her, if not from her, my dreams of love, success, and happiness were being nurtured.

12

the party

Christmas was the best ever. In my heart I felt Joyce and I were on our road to recovery and reconciliation. I achieved the dream of ringing in the new year with a candlelight bath with the woman I love. I was very satisfied with what was happening in my life, although I was letting my goal of becoming a motivational speaker fade for the moment.

One of the married couples in the Carnegie Class threw a party the first week in January. Typically, Joyce pulled away, so I decided to go alone. Michael and Kayne Berry lived in a palatial home. It was the perfect model of the one I was forming in my dreams. I arrived early and found myself parking behind the familiar blue Buick with the same four digits in its plate number as mine. I couldn't help but notice that the ABUSE bumper sticker was gone. Miracles happen, I thought. Sally was growing.

As I entered, I was met by Michael and Kayne, who invited me to make myself at home. I wandered, seeing my dream a reality, when I entered a huge family room, where Sally sat with her two children on the hearth near a roaring fire. My heart throbbed at the vision from my dreams. I sat in a rocker at the far end of the family room and watched Sally with her children. We smiled, of course, but all I wanted to do was watch. As always, a part of me wanted to run, but I knew I was strong enough to stay and make this evening work. As I watched the children, Judy and Tim, I thought it odd Sally brought them to an adult party. I felt the love she had for her children. A mother who has limited time with her children takes them every place she goes.

When Tim became engrossed in a board game, I got down on the floor with him and joined in his play. I glanced at Sally sitting just to my right. She looked contented, shy. She wasn't the Sally I had watched each week in the fellowship hall with a line of admirers waiting to talk to her. Not this Sally. Again, I felt love. Love for the children. Love for me. As Tim and I played, I had a subtle intuition that something was amiss with this little fellow. The ways in which he moved and expressed himself were large and somewhat awkward. We were brothers, whether he realized it or not. I looked in Sally's direction, but my feelings were much too strong for me to communicate. I rose and sat in the rocker at the end of the room.

Entertainment for the evening was a handwriting analyst, who promised to unlock our deepest personal secrets. I didn't have the foggiest what he'd see in my handwriting other than, well, who knew what. I was getting more anxious by the minute. (I had dabbled with a psychic at the flea market once.) We all wrote something on a 3" x 5" card and tossed the cards in a box, then we gathered in a group as cards were drawn and fortunes told. He told me I was destined for greatness. I was in charge of my destiny. I wanted to believe him.

Shortly after he read my card, I went home. All the way home I scolded myself, "You better remember just who in the hell you are! Who, other than a woman with Cerebral Palsy, could love you?" I swore never to get near Sally again.

TV Mania

Greg Shiemke, a member of the Church Of Today's media department, a mutual friend, Larry Murphy, and I started a Cable TV show. Larry was the host. We called the program "Murphy's People." The show ran every week for several weeks until someone complained we did not live in the cable area. Our great show was taken off the air because we lived in the wrong place! Undaunted, we formed Triumph Productions. After three arduous months of politicking, we got the show back on the air.

During our struggle, Larry suggested the three of us go to the support group, Freedom From Fear, at the Church Of Today. Larry and I went on a Thursday evening in late February. Sally was the last thing on my mind that night. When we entered the meeting room, which was set up with twenty round tables with about eight to ten people at each table, my heart leaped. Sally sat alone at one of the rear tables. I went one way and Larry the other. I sat in the chair next to her. She gave me that big sunshine smile.

"Thank you!" she said.

I knew enough about her by this time to know what she meant. It was her way of telling me she felt safe. It was her first time at this support group. When our table was finished, we walked to the door together. Sally asked me if I wanted to Master Mind that night. I looked around for Larry, then asked Sally a question.

"Is there a group you are a member of?"

"No. Just you and me," she replied.

I hesitated, knowing the deep feeling I had been denying since the party at Mike and Kayne's. "Well, OK. We'll go into the chapel."

Master Minding has a strict form. Two people Master Minding shouldn't take more than fifteen minutes. We spent the next hour and a half in the chapel. In the meantime, Larry had been looking for me all over the church. When he found us, he closed the door.

For the next eight weeks, we met faithfully at the bench in the hall. During this time, I kept questioning why this beautiful woman would want to be with me. We shared many things, many thoughts, fears and desires. As I got to know her, I hoped she was getting to know me. I began to understand where she was coming from. Her stories made my life seem like a Sunday School picnic.

During one of our sessions, we Master Minded for me to give another seminar. Sally and I talked about my book. She said she'd like to read it. After I gave her a chapter to read, she asked if she was going to be in it.

"Well, I hadn't thought about it. Maybe I could work you in," I said.

The fact is, I had thought about including her. I hadn't wanted her to know. More accurately, I hadn't truly decided what part she would play. A week later, I decided to write Sally in as my Soul Mate. This was not simply a creative decision. It was something I agonized over and prayed about. Sally just had to be my Soul Mate. I did not seek her, she found me.

The next time we Master Minded together, we saw my book being completed soon. We tossed around ideas for a title since my working title, "Daddy Can't Fix Me," was no longer accurate. This was when something along the lines of "Forgiveness" was discussed. At this same time, I decided it was time for me to do more than merely Master Mind with her. I asked her to go to a movie with me. She accepted, only she said our date would have to wait two weeks. My anxiety was sky high during the wait, fearing she'd cancel. That week was a turning point in the relationship. I decided to give Sally another chapter of my book to read.

"Read this," I said. "It's where I introduce you into the story."

As she read, I watched her face drop. This was it. Now Sally knew how I felt about her. She was subdued the rest of that Master Mind session

The following week, a few days before our movie date, I called Sally.

"What movie do you want to see?" I asked.

"Oh, I didn't know I was to pick the movie."

"Well, I don't think I should do the picking. After all, you are my guest and you should get to pick the movie."

I thought she had reacted strangely. It wasn't until later I learned that no man had ever asked her to make a decision, much less, sought her opinion.

The Friday evening of our date, Sally invited me in before we left for the movie. She offered me a seat on her beautiful couch. As I took a closer look at the doll house I had seen on my first visit, she told me how she and her former husband had built it. Then, she retrieved her family picture album and showed me pictures of herself building it. It seemed strange that she would share these pictures of herself and her husband. I couldn't help but wonder, "Why is this woman sharing all of this with me?" As the conversation wandered, she mentioned she had always dreamed of owning a Jaguar. I told her that when I became a great speaker I would buy her one.

The movie Sally chose was *Jack, The Bear*, a Danny DeVito film about a dysfunctional single-parent household.

Half way through, she said, "Boy, Phil, this movie is sure pushing our buttons!"

"Yeah!" I replied. "But you and I are in recovery from this stuff."

After the movie, Sally didn't want to stop for coffee, and asked me to take her straight home. On the way, I showed her the church I grew up in and how it was similar to the Church Of Today.

"Oh, yeah." she said. "I've been in there."

I pulled my car to the curb, planning to watch Sally get safely into her apartment door. I asked her for a hug, expecting her to leave the car and walk to her door.

"Aren't you going to walk me to the door?" she asked.

"Oh, yeah. Sure."

I stopped the car and went around to open her car door, then walked Sally to her apartment door.

"Well? Aren't you going to give me a goodnight hug and kiss?" she smiled.

I was afraid to hug her because of her abuse history and also because touching a body without Cerebral Palsy was different. It brought out my shame. I hugged her. I was too afraid to kiss her. We parted and I went to my car. I drove home in a flood of memories from all of my other first dates with women with Cerebral Palsy, reliving the ecstasies and the sadnesses at the same time. Opening the door to my town house, I immediately saw the chaos of my existence.

"No way would Sally come into this place the way it looks!"

The Monday following I began to clean out my place. Over the last eight years, leftover junk from my toy train business had accumulated in the hall. It was time to broom it out. I cleaned the entire town house, throwing out stuff I'd been hanging on to for years. I took all the train stuff to Pat & Russ's hobby shop, where I did all the business with the train shows and the, flea market. There was probably a couple hundred dollars of odds and ends altogether.

The Coke And The Jaguar

Continuing to get to know Sally and her to know me proved to be an ongoing challenge. Once, Sally asked me to come to the Singles Club dance at The Church Of Today. The Singles Club sponsored a monthly dance. At the August meeting, Sally was in all of her splendor in one of her flowing formals. I don't dance. But Sally didn't know that. I don't think she gave it a second thought when she asked me to dance with her. I didn't know how to hold her while we were dancing. I was still frightened to touch her. In her strapless gown, there was no place to touch her, except on her bare skin. I enjoyed myself, however, and began to attend the dances on a regular basis.

At a subsequent dance, while Sally wrote out the name tags for guests as they arrived, she looked up at me, without thinking, and asked, "Phil, would you get me a Coke?"

"Sure!" I replied, jumping at the chance to give to her.

In that one brief moment in time, Sally did not see me as a physically disabled man. After I jumped up, I simply asked another friend of mine to pour Sally a Coke and carry it for me to the reception table.

"Here it is!" I boasted, tagging behind.

Sally looked up and immediately recognized what had happened. I could read her face as embarrassment stole her bright smile. Her pain gripped me.

"No! Sally, don't!" I cried. "You asked me for a Coke. Don't think about how I got it for you. Enjoy it. It's all right. I'm human. I want to give. You didn't tell me how to get it. Don't kill my joy of getting you a Coke."

My promise to buy Sally a Jaguar when I became rich came to mind one day while I was at the hobby shop browsing through the quarter-inch scale model cars. I came across a Jaguar model. Russ agreed to trade for the train gear I had brought in. I thought of sending it to her, then decided instead to take it to where she worked. That way I knew she'd get it in one piece. However, I didn't want her to explicitly know it was from me.

It was around 3 p.m. when I arrived at her office building, a medical supply house. One of her coworkers was outside having a cigarette. I asked her to take it to Sally.

"Just tell Sally the car came from the universe," I said.

I got back into my car and drove straight home. When I arrived, Sally had already left a message on my answering machine.

"Hi! This is Sally. I'm leaving this message for the universe. Now, I can say I own a Jaguar. It even came with a great garage! Thank you! Bye!"

There was no doubt the voice on that tape was happy and in love. In fact, to test my grasp on reality, I asked Dick, who had come by to lay new carpeting in my place to listen for himself.

"You wanna hear something?" I asked.

I played the message.

"Man!" he said. "Sounds to me like that woman's in love!"

"Yeah! That's what I'm afraid of!" I responded.

With all of this, I still wasn't sure what was going on between me and Sally. Part of the problem was I wasn't sure what was going on between me and me! I was confused. The entire situation felt strange, precisely because I had never had any relationship with such a beautiful woman who did not have a disability. "Who am I?" I kept asking myself. "Who could believe such a relationship could possibly work?"

If I couldn't handle Sally's beauty and normalcy and Sally couldn't feel settled about my Cerebral Palsy, her children were certainly not bothered by either issue. At the church each Sunday, both Tim and Judy sought me out to say "Hi!" and give me a welcoming hug. I was becoming accustomed to their innocent love and attention.

The At Risk Inner Child

As I felt Sally begin to pull away, I knew she felt she had allowed herself to go to far. As we pushed and pulled at each other around the church with looks and glances, countless chance encounters in doorways and bumping into one another around corners at seminars and other events, I continued to wonder why any woman without a disability would want with a relationship with me. "Not again!" my insides cried.

One night, she walked into the Ram's Horn restaurant near the church as Larry, Greg, and I were Master Minding. I had never seen Sally there on a Monday night, when I was there with my men friends. She sat at a table up the aisle from us. I went over to see her.

"Hi, Sally."

"Phil. I have something important to tell you Thursday."

"Sally, I sure can't be in suspense for four days. Tell me now," I said seating myself, my adrenaline rising.

"OK."

She thought for a moment, then looked at me.

"I want to marry a man like Don Tocco. He's the type of man I want."

In my own defense I said, "I am that type of man."

Then, suddenly out of the blue, in a seemingly unrelated statement, she dropped a bomb.

"Phil, it's my inner child. I want to kill her!"

"Sally! You can't be serious!" I said, dumbfounded.

"I am!"

"Talking that way is the same as talking suicide!" I protested.

"My inner child has gotten me into nothing but trouble."

"Sally, your inner child in the only part of you who can love!" I pleaded with her. Then, I added, "What good is Don Tocco if you kill the only part of you who could love him?"

She was stunned. She rose, asked for a hug, then ran from the restaurant. As I rose to rejoin my group, that damnable empty, dry, and hollow feeling overwhelmed me, like the night I left Janis and Jim at the bar some twenty years earlier. My next reaction was to manipulate the situation to fix everything for my true love that night.

After excusing myself from the Master Mind session, I immediately went home and called Sally. No answer. As I waited to call again in a few minutes, I searched my library for books on the inner child, mostly John Bradshaw books. I found a few references. When I called again, nothing.

With desperate determination, I drove the fifteen miles to her apartment, books in-hand. I rang her bell. No answer. I thought of banging on her window, but my confident inner voice called me off the chase. "She has been here before," it cautioned me, "men chasing her, banging on her window at all hours." Instantly, I felt a sense of peace. Even more, it was some knowing deep inside that she was safe. The universe was protecting her. Feeling the more familiar pangs of rejection I was accustomed to, I drove home.

When I called again from home, she answered. She was still quite upset.

"Thank God you didn't bang on my window. So many men have done that in the past."

At least, a backhanded thank you in the midst of her anger. I was grateful for even that. All else seemed lost, or so I thought.

You Cannot Give Up

The next morning, I called Gary LaLonde.

"Gary, it's all over between me and Sally, whatever the hell we had," I said, half crying.

"What are you saying! Are you going to give up on this one great dream of yours because of one little problem with Sally?"

"This dream, you call it, was the craziest thing I could ever imagine!" I complained.

"Philip, why don't you let God handle this thing? Meanwhile, you have a lot of other things you have to work on. That book of yours isn't going to write and publish itself. Your public speaking career isn't going to happen if you don't work at it. You still have your dreams! Don't let one defeat destroy all of them!" Gary was right. I had to move forward.

In mid-June, I decided to plan another seminar. Ray Genick was disappointed when I let the momentum die after he started me out last year. Maybe it was a way to bring Sally back into my life. I wrote her a business letter, inviting her to sing at the seminar. She called me to say she would be happy to do it. I said I would make a thumbnail of the flyer and send it to her. She reacted quite negatively to my choice of the word "voluptuous" in the copy to describe the beauty and pleasure of her voice. When I apologized and suggested the word "vibrant," she agreed to that.

She stayed on the phone with me for the next thirty minutes, confiding in me I was the only man who had ever asked her for her opinion. As I listened, I began to understand more about Sally. All the while, I was conscious of the fact that business calls do not become thirty-minute intimate conversations unless there is some deeper connection between the two people. Unfortunately, as it turned out, Ray would have nothing to do with having a singer at my seminar, since the event would be sponsored through the university.

PHIL STOP!

I very much wanted to have something positive happen between Sally and I. The only other thing I could think of doing was to send her loving gifts anonymously. Although she kept her distance from me for several weeks, we kept stealing glances at church, or having our coincidental meetings in the halls. I'd walk out of one door; she'd be there. I'd come in a side door; she'd be there. I'd come early; she'd be early. I worked both services in the media department; she would attend both services, continuing her glances over her shoulder at me. I wanted to see her beautiful blue eyes staring at me. I wanted her to smile and speak to me. However, this all felt like a cruel game of torture.

Sometime in mid-August, she came over after a service to where I was sitting. As the crowd filed out, I was expecting some thawing, some progress. It was not to be.

"Phil, stop sending me things in the mail! And, stay away from my children!" she said with cold insistence.

"Well, I think you'd better tell Tim and Judy not to seek me out the way they have been doing these past few weeks!" I quickly responded.

Her cold resoluteness suddenly vanished, replaced with confusion and fear. I hadn't felt such anger since my fight with Joyce, when I wanted to hurt her so she could feel my pain. I thought of adding, "Yeah, they know who Mama's in love with!" But that would have been cruel. She was terribly vulnerable. I never wanted to involve her children in our dispute. I said nothing more. Apparently confused, Sally left the sanctuary.

I spent the rest of the summer concentrating on my seminar and my book. I built my own database and I did all of the work myself. It was a one man show. I wanted it that way. This was my time. My new debut.

Among the 1,200 invitations I sent out, Sally was on the list. I heard nothing from her until a singles meeting about two weeks later. Sally usually makes out name tags as people come into the meeting. When I entered the room, she and Lisa were writing out name tags. I went to Lisa.

"Don't you want Sally to write your name tag?" Lisa asked.

"If she'd like," I said, wanting to avoid embarrassing us both.

Without a word, Sally wrote PHIL in her beautiful proportional handwriting, then stuck the name tag on my shirt. I was pleasantly surprised. I kept my distance during the evening. Toward the end of the meeting, Sally approached me. My fears eased when I saw her radiant smile.

"Good night, Phil," she said as she passed.

In disbelief, I returned, "Good night, Sally."

The next time I saw her in church, I said, "I want to thank you for your warm greeting last Sunday."

"Oh, I didn't want to be rude," she said.

"Rude!" I thought to myself. "What the hell have you been all these months!" I wanted to shout out to her.

The End?

Thinking over the last year, I realized we had celebrated everyone's birthday except Sally's in the Carnegie class. My inner voice told me she never had a birthday party as a child or an adult, so, trusting my inner self,

I decided to really pour out my love for her. Diane Szymanski, who taught Carnegie, also directed the Sunday evening Singles Group. Working with Diane, we planned a surprise birthday party for Sally for the last Sunday in November, during the Singles Group. I arranged to have Diane buy a decorated cake for Sally from me. Of course, as life would have it, two undecorated cakes were delivered!

I arrived for the Singles Group as anxious as ever. Sally was a greeter at the door this night. When I saw her inside the door, I knew there was no other way into the church. I couldn't avoid seeing and speaking with her. She was dressed in a red jumpsuit with a Christmas Tree embroidered on the front. We shook hands.

"You look very charming," I said.

Visions of this woman coming down our spiral staircase in our mansion filtered through my mind.

Each Sunday evening session of the Singles Group consists of some icebreaker exercises Diane uses to get the people to interact with each other. These are followed by a guest speaker. Of all of the topics in the world, tonight's guest speaker was Sue Dahlmann, speaking on "Love Is The Answer."

There are no coincidences in life. I was almost moved to tears as she spoke of knocking down the walls we build between one another because of fears we have nurtured all our lives. It felt like God had given the speech to Sue especially for Sally and me. She spoke of the fears we have of closeness. How when we feel love and become close, we pull away because of our fears. I could see Sally's head nodding up and down in agreement with everything Sue was saying. There was no doubt in my mind this was the reunion I had wanted with Sally for six months.

After the lecture, anxious about the birthday surprise for Sally, I left the room. When I returned, Sally was in tears as everyone sang Happy Birthday to her. She pulled the Happy Birthday lettering from the cake and put it in her purse.

"I never had a birthday," she said between her tears.

Taking a risk, I went up to her. "Happy Birthday, Sally!" I said. "I did it! Sally, I bought the cakes, because I love you!" She looked confused. Her eyes searched mine like a computer searching for a matching file.

"Yeah! I want to tell you something," she said.

I braced myself.

"God has been talking to me about us," she continued.

"Is it good?" I asked, pretending to be excited, when, in fact, I was in fear of rejection. But she did not answer! Quickly, I asked for a hug. Then, someone took a picture of us arm in arm. When I told Sally that a doll was going to come to her during the week, she was all smiles. I was on cloud nine. I had rebuilt the communication we lost. However, I had to discipline myself. I wanted a whole lot more from Sally than I felt she was willing to give at this point. Later, when I asked if I could walk her to her car, she said,

"No."

"Dammit!" I thought, "Phil, you pushed too far again."

Sally said, "Good night," to me as she left the building.

I couldn't wait to send the doll. I wondered if I was looking for the same response I got with the Jaguar as I wrapped this little gift for her inner child in blue wrapping paper with little yellow animals on it. Repeating the delivery procedure I used with the Jaguar, I entered her place of business and looked for someone to take it to her secretly. I wandered through the building, but found no one. When I spotted her coat and hat in a cubical, I left the gift on the desk and ran like a scared rabbit. In my car, I knew this was the worst way I could have handled it.

The note I wrapped with the gift was a letter from the doll addressed to Sally:

Dear Sally:

I'm Amy. I have been sitting on a shelf in this drugstore for many, many months. I have been wanting to become a part of your doll collection. Every time this guy comes by, I keep saying: "Buy me! Buy me!" He said, "No, no. There is no one for me to give you to." I said, "Yes, yes. Your friend Sally wants me." He said, "No! Not from me! She may want you, but not from me." "Yes, she does! She loves you!" I said. "I, don't know," he said. "Yes, sheee doesss!" I said.

The days and weeks went on until I said to him the other day, "Hey, Phil! It's time to buy me for Sally. It's her birthday and I want to be part of her collection. I hate this store shelf. It is lonely here. In her collection I will live with all the other dolls she has. I am magic. I can make her dreams come true." He finally bought me.

Well, Sally, here I am in your hands. That guy is sure loving and caring. He's something special. It must be great knowing him. Now it's time to put me on your shelf with the other dolls. I will make your dreams come true. I can even make toy Jaguars become real someday. You'll see! I love you!"

Happy Birthday!
Amy

Sally's Response

I knew this plan had backfired when I tried calling Sally after I returned home. Her office wouldn't put me through. A week later at church, Les Brown spoke on forgiveness. The week following, I received a long note from Sally in the mail. I read her emphatic "No's" and photocopied pages with highlighted passages from a book on fantasy and co-dependency.

Kamikazi

Sometime later in the fellowship hall, while talking to one of my support group friends, Pete Santoro, who always had an ear for my troubles with Sally, I pointed out to him where Sally was in the room. We were some twenty-five feet away from her. When I saw her look at me and smile, I turned my back to her. As Pete and I continued to talk, she came across the room, brushing against my back as she left the room. Pete's jaw dropped.

"See! See!" I said. "Now, do you believe me?"

Pete didn't know what to say. But he couldn't deny what he had seen with his own eyes. I called these her kamikaze attacks to explain them to my friends.

When this happened again in front of Pete on another occasion a few weeks later, he turned his head and laughed. I asked him what had he was laughing about, as I turned to look and saw Sally streaking away.

"What in the hell does she want?" Pete asked.

"I don't know any more," I said feeling deep sadness and longing for her.

"Well, you better go and ask her, soon!" he recommended.

Later that evening I took the gamble and reestablished communications with Sally. Since that night, we've maintained cordial public communications in the context of church activities. We do not see one another privately…and although we haven't spoken again of our hopes and dreams, I trust she can sense my support for her healing and happiness.

13

loose ends and a new beginning

At the same time that my relationship with Sally was concluding, I continued work on this book, making attempts to contact people I was including in my story, not only to gain verbal permission, but to tie up a few loose ends for myself. For the most part, responses to my calls and letters were positive and cordial. I was especially heartened by the strong encouragement I received from Mark Victor Hansen, Dennis Waitley, Zig Ziglar, Deepak Chopra, Bernie Siegel, Wayne Dyer, Les Brown and other major voices for growth and healing I had met at the Church Of Today and told about my project. The rare negative responses I took at face value. I listening to constructive criticism, and made the appropriate changes as I edited.

Much more difficult were my attempts to make headway with personal contacts. Many friends, relatives and important characters in my life story have passed away; like my friend and mentor, Yale. Others had moved and were out of touch. However, one contact I was able to make created an important closure in my life.

It was that February after the party at Michael and Kayne's, when I played with Sally's son on the floor in front of the hearth. I had begun writing about my relationship with Janis at the same time. It was the first time I began to feel what I was writing. I relived the erotic encounters I had with Janis. I also uncovered a great deal of anger and resentment that still lingered in my heart. I knew I had to forgive both Janis and Jim.

I burst into deep sobs writing about the time I asked Janis how she had learned the ways of pleasuring a man.

The tears unlocked these and many other feelings I had knotted up in my guts. The deep, deep sobbing began to free my spirit. Everything began to fall into place. I realized that writing this book was like constructing a giant jigsaw puzzle. As the pieces of that time moved of their own accord into place, I knew I had to take some physical action. I had to do something. I had to move or become victim again to one of my lonely and depressing moods. I really didn't want to go to my A.A. meeting, so I called Jim and Janis. I had never talked to them since the night at the bar, even though I had seen them once or twice at the MACs after their marriage. My resentment was always too great.

"Hello?" Jim answered.

"Hi, Jim, this is Phil Schmucker."

"Oh yeah, long time no see."

"Yeah, I wonder if you and Janis are going to be home tonight. I thought I'd take a ride over and see you two."

"Sure, come on. We'll be glad to see you."

I had always known where their house was. I had driven past it many times garage sailing in their neighborhood, although I had never stopped. It was cold and windy as I parked in front of the small frame structure. I knocked on the door. To my surprise, a young black woman answered. As I walked into their living room, I was shocked to find Jim in a wheelchair and Janis walking around wearing a helmet. Evidently her epilepsy had progressed. As I found out, Jim had fallen at work and injured his back. The young woman was a live-in caretaker.

As we visited for about an hour-a-half, Jim seemed to be his usual optimistic self, something I always thought was a front for his own pain and anger. As the visit continued, his pain and anger surfaced in many ways. Janis hardly spoke. She appeared to be heavily sedated. Jim told me her doctor was Raymond Bower. (This is the same Dr. Bower who dished out the Librium to me like candy for seventeen years.)

We mainly discussed them and their daily issues. There was no point trying to relate much about me or my new philosophy of life. And since Janis simply sat in her chair and hardly responded to the conversation, there wasn't much I could say to her.

I soon had to leave. I desperately wanted back into the world of reality. I had done what God wanted me to do. I forgave Jim for stealing Janis from me. They seemed to be reconciled and content with their situation.

Walking out the door, the wind blew fiercely and there was a glaze of ice on everything. I walked cautiously to my car and drove off thinking that if I had married Janis, I would have never made it to the Church Of Today. I asked myself how all this stuff was happening. I also asked myself if history was repeating itself with another beautiful woman with blue eyes and blonde hair.

Either in response to my doubts and questions, or in response to the bitterly cold weather, the story of the butterfly came to mind. Another mystery. It carried me to another, warmer and magical time.

Never-Ending Story

As I slowly skated home over the icy roads, I thought about how coming to believe I am a writer has taught me many things about who I am. Now I know why I would sit as a child and watch the "Twilight Zone" or "Alfred Hitchock." The only interesting parts for me being when either Rod Serling or Alfred were doing their narrations. I was fascinated by how they put words together.

I also thought about contemporary writer and TV commentator, Linda Ellerbe, whose trademark phrase is, "And so it goes." I thought, I have come this far in my journey, the rest is up to the God who is within. I felt good that I was coming to know who I am and where I am going. I had a deep sense of gratitude that my transformation was well underway.

I began to think about all of the times I had been driven in a car by someone else, feeling like I was being carried off to some terrible, lonely place. Here I was today at the wheel of my own car…at the wheel of my own life! I am blessed!

Seminar Number Two

Seminar number two went well. More than twenty people attended. I was very satisfied with my presentation and delivery.

I was most pleased by the warm and insightful introduction Don Tocco made, which I include here:

Good evening ladies and gentlemen!

Welcome to an evening of what I believe will be a great deal of excitement and ideas on success, motivation and inspiration.

I'm of the mind that everyone here is already motivated. I really feel that to be true. But inspiration is something more difficult to come by and also more difficult to sustain. I also believe that it is nearly impossible to become inspired by an outside force unless that outside force is itself inspired. But I know this to be true of our guest speaker this evening.

I have known Phil personally for several years. And I have watched Phil transform his life in such an incredible way, unlike so many people who have had great opportunities and have never taken advantage of those opportunities.

Edgar Guest said it another way, and I'd like to share a poem by him called "Sermons We See." He said:

I would rather see a sermon, than hear one any day.
I would rather one should walk with me, than merely show the way.
The eye is a better pupil and more willing and eager.
Fine counsel is confusing, but example always clear.

The best teachers are men and women who live their creeds.
To see the good in action is what everybody needs.
I can soon learn how to do it, if you let me see it done.
I can better watch your hands in action,
    but your tongue too fast may run.

The lectures you deliver may be wise and true,
But I'd rather get my lessons by observing what you do.
I may misunderstand you and that high advice you give,
But there is no misunderstanding of how you act and how you live.

My friends, the person you are going to hear from this evening is…a man who is living his dream, taking charge of his life, overcoming his apparent handicaps, challenges and problems…a man who I am very proud to call my friend. Will you please welcome…Mr. Phil Schmucker!

What is clearly evident by comparing the videos from this and my first talk is the transformation Don so generously pointed out. Sentence by sentence, minute by minute, at my new level of performance, my growth is clear. I can say that I am proud. I can also say that I have raised my sights considerably higher for round three.

A New Spirit Of Giving

By the time Christmas rolled around, I was in an entirely different space. Christmas had once again become a time for unconditional giving and love. The Church Of Today has an entire weekend open house each December. Among other things, it's time for Toys for Tots. As I reviewed all of the toys brought to the church for the children, my heart sank. In the mist of the array of toys were AMY and the JAGUAR! I felt not only the pain of rejection, but a good deal of terror.

"Oh, no!" I thought. "That doll can't be played with. She has a broken leg!" I remembered my new broken train when I was I child. In all the excitement, no one seemed to even notice that the doll was broken. It was only meant to sit on a shelf. I finally got the receptionist Linda Rock, who was also a Carnegie G.A., to write a note and attach it to Amy: "I am Amy. I am magic. I make your dreams come true. Please don't play with me. I am only to sit on a shelf and make dreams come true."

As I looked at Amy with her arm resting on the Jaguar, I prayed, "Oh God, if I am ever to hold Sally again, please bring Amy back to me." Knowing the remote odds of this prayer ever coming true, I went home.

In January, the Wednesday lessons resumed at the Church Of Today. That first Wednesday, Melanie met me as I was hanging up my coat.

"Phil, I think I've got someone you love dearly."

I was confused. But, when Melanie brought Amy to me, I nearly wept. She couldn't have known about my prayer.

"Oh God," I said aloud.

Taking Amy's return as a sign, I brought her home and put her back on my bookshelf, where for weeks she continued to remind me of Sally. I don't remember what it was that unblocked my thinking, but it wasn't Sally Amy was asking for, it was a new home. She wanted me to find her a new home. I needed to let her go. By letting Amy go, once and for all, I could let Sally go. There could be no strings. Nor could I tempt God for signs and promises. I had to let go of the whole thing.

The opportunity came on a Sunday, soon thereafter, when the church announced an auction to raise money for one of the members to have a bone marrow transplant. After a Wednesday lesson, I came home and looked at Amy.

"How about me!" she said. "I need a new home!"

As difficult as it was to relinquish all hope and control, I donated Amy for the raffle. I understand that Amy raised a nice sum for the cause.

HEALING PROCESS

The three-and-a-half years it took to write this book was a healing process for me. Early on, as I wrote in the third person (he, she, they), I expressed a lot of my anger and victimized feelings toward the characters as well as myself. Speaking from the objective third person, as I wrote about my father, I focused on his anger and made him both a tyrant and a fool. On the other hand, he wasn't the saint the world mourned at his funeral. He's still my Daddy. Proudly today, writing in the first person (I), I can say that I still love him and I miss him. With deep sorrow, I mourn the loss of his kind of man in our society: the problem-solving-fix-it-man, the work-till-you-drop-stick-to-it-man, the I'll-be-right-over-and-help-you-out kind of guy, the vulnerable-yet-hard-veneered individualist with the kind of mind and hands that could take a piece of scrap metal or a stack of lumber and make literally anything with lasting value. I mourn the passing of that entire generation.

Those cold, early draft manuscripts also painted my mother to be a servant, a slave, a frustrated perfectionist and moody woman. In essence, she is none of these things, though she is consistent in her impatience with my lack of maturity and struggle for independence. I must become independent, not only for her sake, but for mine. This is where she is coming from, and we both know that. Neither of us thought it would take me all 52 years of my life and more. What a burden for her! She carried all of my Daddy's hopes for me when he was alive. She carries them, still, as I continue to demanded much from her. In all these years, my Ma has never said, "No."

For myself, I remain a Peter Pan. At times I am out of control, not simply due to my Cerebral Palsy, but due to my strong inner child who insists on doing the right thing as I see it and being clear in all my dealings with others. I do not care to be "adult" in the clever or manipulative ways of the world.

In fact, I'm labelled screwy by others when I insist upon self-reliance for handicapped people. It still pains me deeply to think that each yearly crop of handicapped persons is being shunted from the mainstream at places like the League For The Handicapped or politicized into some irrational lobby group. Actually, it pains me to hear of any child or adult being "tracked" into a life that denies them their dreams. I'm called radical when I express anger at how the medical establishment used handicapped children like me to test Librium, and kept me hooked for twenty years, and continues today to impress upon society that "taking the edge off" with Prozac, or some other numbing chemical, is the right thing to do.

In my transformation, I am learning to embrace the light and the dark, the pain and the no-pain, the ups and the downs. Swings between extremes are still too wild in my life to claim that I am in control, but I no longer need to modify them with drugs or alcohol. In contrast, once I was clear of drugs, I learned through the Church Of Today that I could create entirely new and productive paradigms about my reality. I remember being told when I described the outline of my book that it had no ending. I never for one second believed it made any difference. I now know that we all have the power to not only rewrite (rethink) the past, but to write (recreate) the future. Writing my biography was just such an exercise at stretching my creative powers. I have not only written my life story. I am now writing a new beginning to my future!

To Publish

Part of my healing process during the writing of this book involved driving to Ann Arbor, Michigan, to join a group of people who chant ancient mantras. Larry Murphy introduced me to this group led by Bob and Jean Bedard. When I told Jean about my book, she told me about her desktop publishing company. After a long talk with Don Tocco, I realized I would have to self-publish. What's more, he pledged the first thousand dollars!

Armed with Don's $1,000 of encouragement, I called Ralph Grzecki, an associate minister at the Church Of Today, who also encouraged me and gave me the phone number of David Lindsey, an entrepreneur and self-publisher. David suggested I call Diane Harper, a graphic designer. After she read my manuscript, Diane called to ask if she could to pass it on to a writer/producer friend of hers, Ed Penét, who not only writes films, videos, stories, plays and poetry; but has worked both as a book and magazine editor. Ed had also just sold the rights to a book to Hollywood. I agreed to let Ed see the manuscript. Meanwhile, I kept writing letters to friends and motivational speakers I knew to raise the money to self-publish my book.

In August, my Uncle Leo (my mother's brother), passed away. I went to the church in my new suit and tie to pay my respects and to show off the new Phil. I was the only nephew in suit and a tie on this hot, steamy, rainy August evening. Also at the church was Emmett Webb, whom I hadn't talked to in many years. When I told him about the book I was writing, he seemed interested. I asked him for a thousand dollars, like I was asking almost everyone else.

"What would the return on my investment be?" he asked.

I wasn't prepared for that.

"Suppose I gave you the whole twenty thousand?"

I hadn't thought of that, either!

"I know the book will be a best seller!" I responded.

"Can you guarantee ten to one return!"

"Sure!" I replied with all the confidence I could muster.

With that, Emmett committed to an initial thousand dollars. When I left the church that night, I had a very powerful inner knowing that Emmett would give me the whole twenty thousand.

By October, Ed had read the manuscript and agreed to do a major edit within my budget. He and I began meeting to discuss his ideas to rewrite in the first person, condense the material and add much more personal detail. Ed and I also met with Diane to discuss the design and publishing process in order to gauge the total costs of self-publishing the book. Ed and Diane were enthusiastic about doing the book, including a follow-up screenplay. Ed also agreed to do the work piecemeal as I raised the funds.

My inner voice was telling me to call a meeting that included Emmett, Diane, Ed, and myself. We soon agreed to meet at Emmett's home. I was nervous, to say the least, waiting for Ed and Diane to arrive. Waiting has never been one of my finer attributes. While Diane and Ed explained to Emmett what they felt needed to be done, including the timing and the costs involved, I sat there remembering the drive home from Uncle Leo's funeral, knowing that Emmett would agree to foot the entire bill for the book. That's exactly what happened! The deal was made that night, and within two weeks papers were written up and signed.

As I've written, during the six months of rewriting and editing, I felt myself being healed, especially in regard to my feelings about my father. For the first time, through Ed's recasting of the book in the first person from the third person, I could see and feel the helplessness and hopelessness my father felt in my early life. Many times, as Ed read the rewritten manuscript aloud to me, I balled like a baby. The forgiveness I needed to heal my woundedness was coming through.

The book and my healing process also contributed to a great healing between myself and Joyce. After reading excerpts, she, too, could see, feel and understand the hell we were living trying to put meaning into our marriage.

Recently, Joyce and I went out to a comedy club, where an improvisation team asked for character suggestions. I blurted out, "Cerebral Palsy!" on impulse as a stunt. It shocked Joyce. The comedian who picked up on it was hilarious. As he stumbled into the party of "misfits," which was the premise, there he was with an ice cream cone stuck on his forehead. Out in the audience, Joyce and I were laughing at our pain. We had walked into a new light!

It is very clear to me that my life is a gift from God. I forgive.

EXCELSIOR!

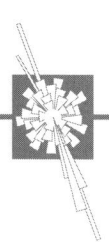

Patricia appears to be upset.

"This isn't very fair to the reader."

She gets no response.

"I mean, it doesn't end!" she persists.

"What ends is a great deal of pain and frustration. And what begins is an openness and a trust that will blossom. You'll see," says the voice of Wisdom from behind the back of the white leather overstuffed chair.

"So, what should I tell Transcription?" she asks, as yet unconvinced.

The chair turns slowly around.

God says, "Tell them, thank you for a job well done. It is finished. For now."

"That's it?"

"That's it," God responds.

"We were all speculating on how it would end," mumbles Patricia.

"Think of it not as an end, but as a beginning, Patricia."

"I hate cliffhangers!" Patricia blurts out.

God walks to his panoramic overview of the universe. After a moment of thought, God turns to Patricia.

"Then, think of it this way. Billions of stars, billions of souls. Each atom alive with the creative spirit of the Creator. There are no magic formulas, no secrets, no incantations, no keys to the kingdom ... indeed, no kingdom! There is only being! Being in Me and Me in being."

Patricia listens, knowing there is more.

"What concerned me about Phil were the concerns I have for you, Patricia, for every morsel of being in creation. I have no interest in meddling or granting special graces and favors to him over anyone. I have no interest in helping him find a Soul Mate. That is his quest to pursue or not as he chooses."

"Not fair!" Patricia says to herself.

"To choose! That's what I wanted to see in him. To choose, to act, and to be responsible for the good and the bad that flow from his actions. That's what I wanted to see. I Who made the Light. I Who made the Dark. I Who made all that is in between. I want Phil to be heir to it all! You don't think I'm granting him too much, do you?" God chuckles, stealing a look at Patricia.

Patricia smiles and relaxes at this display of Divine humor.

"For better *and* worse. In sickness and in health. He can have it all or in any blend his chooses. He was blind and now he sees. I take that, Patricia, to be my highest satisfaction. He who truly sees ... sees Me. That sight is the purest form of prayer."

Silence.

God turns to give Patricia a long look.

"Oh! Yes. I agree, of course. I'll get the word out to Transcription. Anything else?"

"Thank you, Patricia. Well done."

Patricia exits the office.

As God regards the panorama of the universe, God thinks aloud.

"Remember, Phil ... when you and your Soul Mate departed from my office, even as you and Janis parted in such painful silence, and as you boldly parted with Amy, Phil ... you became, each time, a little more free. Do you see that? You see that now, don't you? Phil? Can you see Me?"

THE END

to order more books

If you would like to order more books, please send this order form (or a photocopy of it), along with your check or money order — no cash or CODs please, to:

    Express Motivations
    Philip Schmucker
    15635 Sabre Lane
    Fraser, Michigan 48026

Please send_____copies of "I Forgive – Miracle of Transformation" to:

Name:_____

Name of church or organization:_____

Address:_____

City:_____State:_____Zip:_____

Total number of copies_____@ $12.95 each_____

       Michigan Residents add 6% Michigan Sales Tax_____

          Plus $1.50 each for Postage and Handling_____

          Total amount of Check or Money Order_____

to order more books

If you would like to order more books, please send this order form (or a photocopy of it), along with your check or money order — no cash or CODs please, to:

    Express Motivations
    Philip Schmucker
    15635 Sabre Lane
    Fraser, Michigan 48026

Please send_____copies of "I Forgive – Miracle of Transformation" to:

Name:_____

Name of church or organization:_____

Address:_____

City:_____State:_____Zip:_____

Total number of copies_____@ $12.95 each_____

        Michigan Residents add 6% Michigan Sales Tax_____

          Plus $1.50 each for Postage and Handling_____

           Total amount of Check or Money Order_____